BREAKING THE CODE

A Father's Secret, a Daughter's Journey, and the Question That Changed Everything

KAREN FISHER-ALANIZ

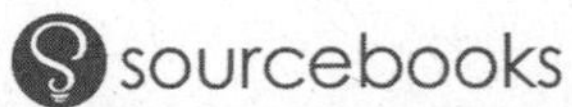

This book is a memoir. It reflects the author's present recollections of her experiences. Some names and characteristics have been changed, some events have been compressed, and some dialogue has been re-created.

Published by Sourcebooks, Inc.
P.O. Box 4410, Naperville, Illinois 60567-4410
(630) 961-3900
Fax: (630) 961-2168
www.sourcebooks.com

Library of Congress Cataloging-in-Publication Data

Fisher-Alaniz, Karen.
Breaking the code : a father's secret, a daughter's journey, and the question that changed everything / Karen Fisher-Alaniz.
p. cm.
1. Fisher, Murray William 2. Fisher, Murray William—Correspondence. 3. World War, 1939–1945—Personal narratives, American. 4. World War, 1939–1945—Campaigns—Pacific Area. 5. World War, 1939–1945—Cryptography. 6. Sailors—United States—Biography. 7. Fathers and daughters—United States—Biography. 8. Fisher-Alaniz, Karen. I. Title.
D767.9.F56 2011
940.54'8673092—dc23
[B]

2011027566

Printed and bound in the United States of America.
VP 10 9 8 7 6 5 4 3 2 1

BREAKING THE CODE

To my father, Murray William Fisher

And in memory of
my grandmother, Ruby Lavinia Fisher,
and my father's comrade, Mal

Contents

Preface

Regulations required that messages containing communication intelligence be destroyed, and as a consequence, no record of the many successes due to this intelligence can ever be compiled.—Vice Admiral C.A. Lockwood in a letter to the Chief of Naval Communications, June 17, 1947.

The journey we embarked on almost ten years ago was a simple one: my father was suffering from nightmares and flashbacks, and I wanted to help him. But as time went on, I learned that in order to help him, I needed to know more about the war.

I am not a historian. I simply learned what was pertinent to helping my father and, eventually, to writing the book you hold in your hands. My father's little corner of the war is just that—a tiny piece of a very intricate puzzle. As such, the information contained here is by no means a complete history of the war or even of his part in it.

It is simply a story, told over time, to the most unlikely of people—me.

A Word about Words

When I originally transcribed more than four hundred pages of my father's letters, I did so with meticulous accuracy. I spelled things just as he had, even if it was incorrect (which was rare). I made a note if he wrote something and then crossed it out. The last half of his letters were typewritten in caps, so I even went so far as to hit the caps lock on my computer. However, when the project evolved into a book, some changes had to be made.

In order to keep the story moving, I have left out sections that were redundant or not relevant to the overall story. Where grammar was concerned, I only intervened if an error made the meaning unclear (most of the time, it was a simple issue, like taking out a dash and replacing it with a period or comma). I did, however, choose to keep the spelling of some words, such as "tho" and "tonite," to retain the letter's original flavor. I have also kept some of my father's words that are considered offensive by today's standards.

Obviously, my father did not keep copious notes in the middle of a war. As is the case with most memoirs, I have filled in conversations from memory, notes, and from knowing the cadence and personality of our speech. Every effort was made to stay true to what happened.

I have watched my father struggle over the past ten years to put memories together that his mind had clearly protected him from for more than fifty years. The memories came back in bits and pieces, often seemingly unrelated. It was in the writing of the book that I was able to piece the whole story together. Thus, the chronology of the book does not necessarily reflect the chronology of how his memories came back. As the author of this book, I take sole responsibility for any unintended errors.

Acknowledgments

To my family, who helped me do the research for the book and then stood back and made me look smart. We know who the real smart ones are: to my mother, Bettye Fisher, for her relentless prayers; my husband, Ric; and my children, Danielle, Micah, and Caleb, who sacrificed so much.

To my friends, who encouraged me along the way. To Shirley Pope Waite, my mother's friend, who years ago encouraged me to write. To my friend since childhood, Kristin Dewey, who always believed in me. To Randy LaBarge, who said, "This is a story that has to be told. What can I do to help?" Your belief in my father and his story breathed new life into the book. To Christine Koehler, your faith in me was contagious.

To the many people who prayed for this project. To Chuck Hindman, for writing the memorial for Mal and for encouraging us to create an intentional time of remembrance. To Ed and Nila Hamshar, for listening.

To Master Chief Intelligence Specialist (Surface Warfare), David L. Murdock U.S.N. (Ret.), a stranger who became a friend. Thank you for lending me your expertise in naval intelligence. You were a lifeline when I needed one.

To Lt. Col. Richard Dixon, U.S. Army (Ret.), who whispered

in my ear, "You have to get this book published. It's not just for your father. It's for all of us."

To Dr. Jauhiainen, "Dr. J.," MD, for understanding PTSD and its impact on my father. And for taking the time during your busy workday to listen to his story.

To the strangers who shook my father's hand and thanked him for his service. Words can never express how important each instance was to him.

To the veterans of wars both past and present. Thank you for your sacrifices that continue long after you return. You are not forgotten. Your story matters.

To the family and friends of veterans, for welcoming our heroes home and for helping them put the pieces of their lives back together long after the homecoming celebration is over.

To the Pacific Northwest Writer's Association for putting together a conference that was instrumental in getting this work published.

To all of the wonderful and passionate people at Sourcebooks. And especially to my editor, Peter Lynch, for believing in this book.

CHAPTER ONE

Healing Waters

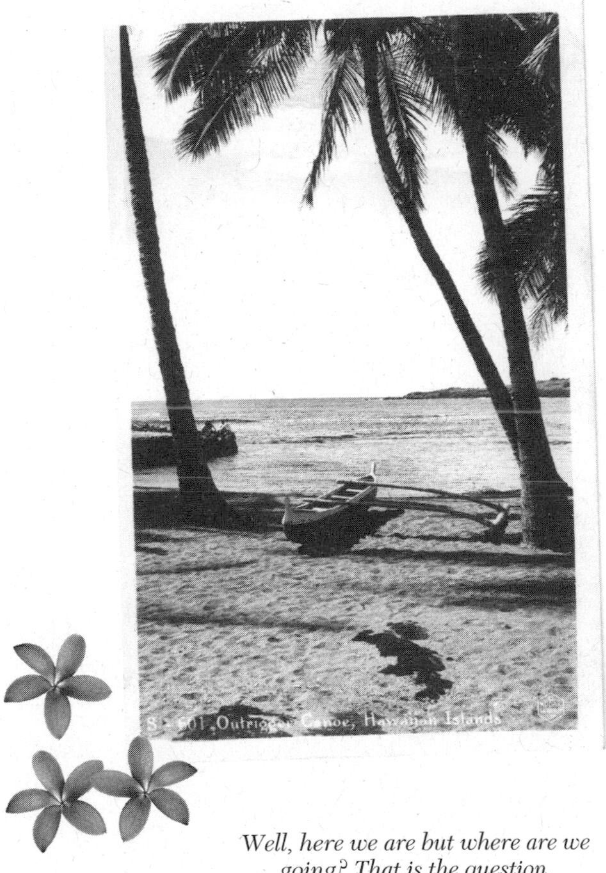

Well, here we are but where are we going? That is the question.
—January 9, 1945

He stood at the end of the pier watching the petals drift out to sea. He leaned on his cane. No longer the young sailor he'd once been, he was an old man now, something his comrade, his friend, never got to be. The red and white petals followed an unseen path, becoming tiny specks in a vast ocean—an ocean that, during the war, held only sorrow and loss. But now those same waters were a place of healing.

"Never good-bye," he said softly. "Never good-bye."

CHAPTER TWO

A Line in the Sand

It's sure tough alright but it's going to be worth it. I've learned more about the Navy in the past two days in the barracks room lecture than in two months at home.—April 28, 1944

PASSING IN REVIEW
There's pageantry aplenty each Saturday afternoon at Farragut as the bluejackets pass in review. Every patriotic heart beats a little faster as Old Glory parades past, fluttering proudly in the afternoon sun. It makes you wish that Schickelgruber and Hirohito could see it too, cause then they'd sense the strength of unconquered America and the spirit of free men!

I always knew my father had been in a war. But as a child it was of little importance to me. I had bicycles to ride, friends to play with, and trees to climb.

He would tell us stories about the war. He was in the Navy and stationed at Pearl Harbor a few years after it was bombed in 1941. He spent his days working in an office. On liberty, he went to the movies or exploring with friends. These were the stories he told, which were never terribly interesting. And although he didn't tell them on a regular basis, during our childhood years, my sisters and I heard each one many times.

It would always begin the same way—with something that sparked the memory—and then the retelling would begin. The details never changed. His memory never wavered. Each story had a beginning, middle, and end.

My sisters and I, all born years after the war, must have had some innate sense that these stories were important, even sacred. Following my mother's lead, we stopped whatever we were doing to listen. We didn't interrupt or ask questions. We never informed him that we'd heard this one before.

When he got to the end, he would simply go back to what he'd been doing. Then weeks, months, and even years would pass without a single story being told. If I'd ever written them down, I'm sure there would have been only eight or ten stories overall. New stories were never added.

In my teens, my patience for the repeated stories ran out. When I heard a story coming, I looked for the nearest exit. I rolled my eyes or sighed loudly, hoping he'd get the hint. He never did. Once the story began, nothing could stop him from finishing it. To me, the stories were just that: stories, ancient history. I filed them away with the stories of my grandfather walking to school in a blizzard. They were irrelevant, intangible. As I got older, he told them less and less.

What I didn't know then was that the stories he told weren't the whole story at all. They were an abbreviation. He told the version that fit comfortably into his middle-class life—the version where everyone lived happily ever after. But more than anything, he told the version that didn't hurt and didn't require answering questions. The rest of the story, the whole and true story, would have remained untold. But one day, many years later, in a single moment, everything I thought I knew about my father's war was turned inside out. We didn't know it then, but it was the first step on a long journey we'd take together.

April 27, 2002, was my father's eighty-first birthday. We gathered at my parents' house—the small, but sunny home I'd grown up in—for the party. Our family is small and most of us live in the same small town. When we're all together, we take up the three comfortable chairs (recliner reserved for Dad), one sofa, and the hearth in front of the fireplace; a few kids sit on the carpeted floor. Although the house has gone through many transformations, one of which was the floor-to-ceiling brick fireplace, my father never seemed to change.

He had looked virtually the same all of my life. The only thing that changed was the color of his now gray hair, and probably the prescription for his eyeglasses. He was one of those people that you go to high school with and then see thirty years later and they truly haven't changed; they've just gotten a little older.

After dinner, as everyone settled into comfortable conversation, Dad slipped away. A few minutes later, I looked up to see him in the middle of the room. With a nod of his head, he gestured away from the crowd. I looked around to see who he was nodding at but quickly realized he was looking at me.

No one seemed to notice when, in the midst of his celebration, we went to the sunroom just two steps down from the living room. The cathedral windows that let light pour in from three sides, coupled with my mother's abundant house plants, made it feel more like an atrium. Dad sat on the curved sofa that hugged one corner of the room and patted the seat next to him. When I sat down, he placed two binders on my lap, one black and one blue.

"What's this?" I asked.

"Letters," he said. "I wrote them to my folks during the war. You can throw them in the garbage or burn them if you want. I don't care."

"Dad! Why would you say that?" I asked.

He didn't answer.

I opened one of the two-ring binders to find letters written in my father's notoriously tiny handwriting. I skimmed them and asked a few questions. But no matter how general the question, my father had no answer. I read aloud, a line or two at first and then a whole paragraph.

"I wrote that?" he asked. "I don't remember writing that."

With that, he quietly but firmly drew a line in the sand. He was on one side; I was on the other. My questions unanswered, I wanted to implore, "What *is* this? All these years you've had these and you didn't tell me? Why? Tell me now. Tell me everything." I stepped over the line cautiously, looking into his eyes, but then I backed up in silence, deafening silence. I retreated to the other side of that line. And then he bowed his head and walked away.

Alone that night, my family sleeping peacefully, I sat in near darkness. Only a small table lamp with beaded fringe illuminated the notebooks on my lap. I ran my hand across the weathered notebooks and cried. I cried for what I didn't know. I cried for all the times I didn't care and didn't listen. And I cried for the years those letters remained tucked away. Why had he kept them a secret for more than fifty years? There had to be a reason.

About six months prior to his birthday, he had become depressed. He seemed to be driven to watch war movies that were more and more graphic. Bookshelves were filled with WWII books he'd read, often in one day. It was then that I began asking him questions about the war. All he told me were the same stories I'd heard before. But now I wondered about these letters. Was there something in them that he wanted me to know?

I opened the notebook and began reading. The first letter was from boot camp in Farragut, Idaho. Every letter began with the same salutation, "Dear Folks."

4/28/44

Dear Folks,

First of all, please send about 10 airmail stamps (8 centers) and a couple of small packages of writing paper with envelopes, a pad would be best. So many things happening I can't even start. Arrived at about 1730 yesterday, got skinned alive. In other words, my wavy locks are almost a minus quality. Have two stripes on my lower sleeve but guess they are just saving time as we all get that when we graduate from here. The traveling kit is just what the doctor ordered but could only have one bottle in it—that's OK tho. We are all in the United States Navy Reserves now. I passed the physical again with 100% so I am resigned to the fact that I'm OK. Spent most of the day at physical exam and getting clothes, shots etc. The shots were the very least of the trouble—didn't even notice when they did it, but tonite left upper arm's sore. But at that not so bad as when Gerry or Ray [brothers] swats me one on the shoulder. It's sure tough alright but it's going to be worth it. I've learned more about the Navy in the past two days in the barracks room lecture than in two months at home. Will Write. Write real soon, Murray

My father was a good writer. I don't know why this surprised me, but it did. In the short letter home, he'd managed to paint a picture of boot camp that danced vividly in my imagination.

And his quirky sense of humor was there too. I went to bed that night hopeful and excited. It was as if I'd boarded a plane and would be told where I'd be going mid-flight; I didn't know the place, but was excited to experience it.

The next night I read a few more letters, and the next a few more. Soon my nights fell into a routine. After tucking the kids into bed, I put on my pajamas and fuzzy purple slippers. I shimmied a notebook off of the overstuffed bookshelf next to my bed, and sat down on the sofa with a cup of spiced tea. Carefully turning each thin page, I became immersed in the story unfolding before me. With each letter I read, I learned more about the man my father was in his younger days. And although I didn't realize it then, with each letter I came closer to discovering secrets my father had buried for decades.

CHAPTER THREE

Between the Lines

Had to work a little today. Went into an office and stapled sheets of papers together for three hours. What a life. Wonder if I'll ever see a radio any more.—January 15, 1945

As vivid as my father's descriptions in his letters were, I found myself wanting to know more. So, after reading the first few letters, I stopped by my parents' house.

Dad looked up from his throne, a burgundy recliner. He put a scrap of paper in the book he was reading and balanced it on a pile of others. Looking at what was in my hand, he raised his eyebrows.

"What do you have there?" he asked.

"Your letters," I said.

"Why are you carrying those old things around?" he asked.

"Well, I've been reading them and—" I started.

"Why would you want to do *that*?" he interrupted.

"Do what?" I asked.

"Read them. Why would you want to read them?" he asked.

"I don't know," I said. "I guess because they're a part of our family history."

"That's not history," he argued. "That's just a bunch of old letters."

"Dad, this *is* history," I countered.

The quiet of the room encircled us. I leaned forward and nervously tucked one foot under me. I looked around. My mother, who had greeted me at the door, was gone. She hadn't offered her usual hospitality, a piece of last night's dessert or a chocolate she'd kept hidden from my father.

"Dad," I said. "Reading your letters made me curious about some things and I have a few questions for you."

"It's been too long," he said.

He rested his head on the back of the recliner and closed his eyes.

"I don't remember anything," he said.

Silence ensued. I waited. *Stick to the facts*, I told myself.

I took a deep breath.

"How far was Farragut from Dayton?" I asked.

"What?" he asked.

He opened one eye and then closed it again.

"You were in boot camp at Farragut Naval Base in Idaho, right?" I continued. "So how far was that from your parents' home in Dayton?"

Dad opened his eyes and gazed at the ceiling.

"About a four-hour drive I guess," he said. "Of course we didn't have the fast cars and the nice highway that they have now."

He paused.

"I was one of the lucky ones though," he said. "Boot camp was close to home for me. Most guys were sent halfway across the country. But I was stationed close to home. Then when boot camp was over, I got to do my training there too. Did I ever tell you about my first day of radio school?"

I shook my head. I felt like a little girl again, hearing one of his stories. But this time, I wasn't looking for the nearest exit. This time, I hoped the moment wouldn't end.

In the classroom that first day, the instructor quickly tapped out a simple Morse code message. My father already knew the code, having just left his job as a railroad telegrapher. So while his classmates worked feverishly deciphering the message, Dad watched a bird perched on a branch outside the window. The instructor thought he'd caught him off task.

"What was the message I just sent?" he barked.

When my father was able to tell him the correct answer, the instructor stood dumbfounded. After class, he excused my father from the rest of the course.

Each subsequent class that day would follow the same pattern; the instructor would give students a pre-test, never expecting anyone to pass it. But my father passed time and again. By the end of the day, he was excused from six of the seven daily classes. The only one that remained was Navy Procedure, a mandatory class for all radioman candidates. Dad now had only a one-hour course each day, and seven hours with nothing to do, so when a Chief Specialist pulled him aside and asked him if he wanted to learn a different kind of code, *just for fun*, my father was happy to have something to do to pass the time.

It seemed informal enough, just one serviceman to another. The code was one based on the Japanese language. It was called Katakana or Kana for short. They sat across from each other in a classroom filled with communications equipment. People walked by now and then but paid no attention. Neither teacher nor student shared any personal information, other than what they'd done in their civilian life; the student had worked for the railroad and his teacher had worked for the FBI.

Day after day, my father learned the complicated code that had about 125 characters, versus the mere thirty-two he was used to. At first he struggled a bit, but soon he caught on and he even found that he was good at it. But when radio school ended, so did his one-on-one lessons. It was all just for fun and he was glad he'd had something to fill the long hours.

After graduating from radio school, he spent a few weeks at home before his parents drove him to the airport, travel orders in hand. He flew to San Francisco and then took a bus across the Bay Bridge to Treasure Island, a small island between San Francisco and Oakland. He knew—everyone knew—that if you were sent there, you were going overseas.

He lived on the military base for a few weeks before receiving further travel orders. This time, he wasn't told where he was going, only that he would travel by ship. He left the sunny California shore aboard a ship with about twenty of his classmates from radio school and hundreds of other servicemen.

Dad continued to write letters to his folks, though now he was ordered not to tell his family where he was going or how he was getting there. All outgoing correspondence was censored, but he quickly learned the tricks to getting around those censors.

His family and friends had received letters first from Farragut Naval Base, and then from Treasure Island, California. But letters coming *to him* were slow. The mail was always behind, following him from one new address to another.

It was at this time that he made a promise to himself. Having left his small farming town behind, he was now homesick for the first time in his life. He vowed that when he finally *did* begin receiving letters, he would write back within twenty-four hours.

At home that night, I thought about the story my father had told me. Perhaps he had told me this story before, but it had never seemed so vibrant, so real, as it had this time. It was a small thing perhaps. But it was a start.

I began reading his letters again, this time with a better understanding of who he was then and how he ended up so far from home.

CHAPTER FOUR

Across the Years

Arrived at about 1730 yesterday, got skinned alive. In other words, my wavy locks are almost a minus quality.
—April 28, 1944

s I made my way through the next batch of letters, I was struck by the enthusiasm in my father's writing after he got his orders to ship out.

January 9, 1945

Dear Folks,

Well, here we are but where are we going? That is the question. So darned many things have happened since my last letter that I don't know where to start. In fact everything is censored so can't say much of anything. We can say that we had an uneventful trip but not as smooth as the plane trip to Frisco. In fact I was very squeamish all the way. The minute we sighted land tho I came right out of it and went on deck. Aside from being a little weak I'm feeling like a million. Oh yes, we can also say we are at [cut out by censors]—Just get all the books you can on the Hawaiian Islands and you'll know as much about it all as I do.

I'm just bubbling over with enthusiasm for the place. That's sure not like my Navy career prior to this time. But it's just like another dream—off that darned ship and on this plane. We have everything around us here you ever read or heard about the islands. I'll try to send some souvenir booklets. You know, I'd like to visit or even live here in peace time. Here it is January and during the day it's just like spring at home. Just a little on the warm side, but seems like a light breeze blowing most of the time. Then at night it's real cool. Use just one blanket but I don't really need it and sleep like a log. This place is just like a rest cure. It's sure not a disappointment from what I've ever heard of the islands. Everything's green and fertile. You never see any brown dirt. It's all a brick red color and tracks into everything. Really is fertile tho. Seems like everything grows in it.

We have the best food here since I've been in the Navy. And plenty of it. We have nice clean barracks—all kinds of facilities for entertainment, even an outdoor theatre where you sit on a grassy bank and watch the show.

I'm still swaying around as if I were still aboard ship. Sure hope I can get an island base somewhere. Haven't had any work to do yet and did nothing aboard ships. I'm beginning to think we just wasted our time in school. Nothing to do with radio yet.

Well, we lost some more of the gang yesterday. Some of them went on from here on the transport. Took us off alphabetically to the Mc's and so that cut us in two again. Won't be much of the original gang left when we get to our final destination.

Haven't had any liberties yet but don't care at all except maybe to see a couple of the cities. It's so nice and green and quiet right here that I don't even care to see a city for awhile.

Keep writing and often. Use this new address until further notice and either send airmail or V-mail. Send all the fotos you can get your hands on. Maybe when I get settled a little I can send for the whole album.

Well, you know right about where I am, how I am, and all about Oahu now, so everyone should be happy—including the censors. Of course still have no idea where or when from here except doubt very much if we go east (fat chance).

Write and tell everyone else to. Lots of Love, Murray

I laughed to myself. I found it funny that with a war in full swing he was talking about the green grass. You see, my father had always had the most plush and green lawn in his neighborhood. He was obsessed with having the greenest, thickest grass. I don't know if he was competing with the neighbors or only with himself. As kids we could never leave anything on the lawn for fear that it might leave a burn mark, which in southeastern Washington with temperatures often in the nineties was a real possibility. He studied the best times to water and timed his waterings perfectly. He even invented a lawn mower.

Yes, I was the only kid I knew whose friends came over to watch her dad mow the lawn. He had built an electric lawn mower, long before they were produced and sold. It was low to the ground and required no handles. Operated by remote control, a long, thick electrical cord followed it across the yard. It mowed a long strip and then quickly turned to do the next. He'd sit on the front porch, elbows resting on his knees, and mow the lawn.

It was amazing to me, as I read the letters, to see pieces of the father I knew in this young man who in other ways seemed so different. I dove back in, wanting to know more.

Jan 15, 1945

Dear Folks,

Just a line tonite—seems funny to be writing just as if I were in Helix or somewhere else. Nothing more going on here than there either. Of course it's all settled after the little bout three years ago [the bombing of Pearl Harbor]. Lots of Orientals all over the place mixed with soldiers, sailors and marines from all over the world. It's quite a place but I can see it would get tiresome after a while.

Had to work a little today. Went into an office and stapled sheets of papers together for three hours. What a life. Wonder if I'll ever see a radio any more.

Well I have my choice of three movies, a stage show, or a boxing match—think I'll see the stage show.

Still no mail—saw one guy get 31 letters all at once the other day. Hope I do the same soon. I doubt if they get the mail forwarded from Treasure Island for quite a while.

Guess I better take off and see a show. Goodnight. Love, Murray

After reading the letter, I paused. Something seemed different. In the course of six days, he went from wanting to live on Oahu during peacetime to feeling it could get tiresome. The hopefulness of his first few letters was quick to fade. Was that because of the war or simply because he was away from home?

Jan 22, 1945

Dear Folks,

Just a line or two—finished first day of school. It's just a refresher course in everything we had before, mostly just to pass the time I'd guess. The instructors don't hang around much and nobody studies much.

Weighed myself in Waikiki the other day—guess what? I weighed 150 pounds. This climate must agree with me. I eat meals and between meals continuously. Even the gang are beginning to have hopes for me.

They announced we could send laundry to the officers' laundry today, so I bundled up all my dirty clothes and sent them off.

Also my address is Ad.Com.Phib.Pac., which is merely an abbreviation for Administrative Command Amphibious Pacific—which is just what we wanted to stay out of. However seems like the entire Navy including larger ships come under amphibious forces now so nothing to get excited about.

Better get busy. Write. Love, Murray

With this letter though, there was no denying the change; he seemed more listless, less forthcoming about everything he was experiencing. The last paragraph of his letter made me think for the first time about my grandmother, who was receiving the letters. My father was in Amphibious Forces, but he seemed to be trying to soften that fact.

A quick Internet search revealed the reason. The Amphibious Forces, or Amphibs for short, had a very high mortality rate. If your submarine was hit, you wouldn't survive. He was, I figured, trying to spare his mother unnecessary worry.

I wondered, though, if my grandmother saw through my father's words as I had. And if she had, I knew she would have been overcome with the same feeling I had now: that something about his letters wasn't quite right.

I sat in the dim light of the living room and looked across the street at my neighbor's house. Their children tucked in hours ago, only the faint glow of perhaps a nightlight crept across the walls of the sleeping house as I finished reading my last letter for the night. Up the street a bit was a place in the road where there was too much distance between streetlights. It was a piece of darkness that seemed out of place. I sat alone with my thoughts and alone with the unanswered questions. I struggled to understand. Had my father purposely kept the letters a secret? And if so, why?

Over the years, I'd read magazine articles about veterans who came home from the various wars unable to cope. Plagued by terrible memories, they'd never been able to resume any semblance of a normal life. That wasn't true for my father. He came home from the war and went on with his life, seemingly unaffected.

But then, less than a year ago, at the age of eighty, something changed. My mother first noticed it shortly after the tragedy of September 11, 2001. He was distant and disengaged from the life that swirled around him. He was reading WWII books and watching hours of war movies.

She was concerned and so was I, so I started to ask questions.

He responded to each one with a slightly different variation of the same answer. The war stories he told were the same ones I'd heard all my life. They were about the adventures afforded young men away from home. He told us about going on liberty and goofing off with friends. He told us about Mary's Steakhouse and the Waikiki movie theater. This was my father's war. He served his country from behind a desk. It wasn't an exciting story to tell, but it takes all kinds of soldiers and sailors to support the war effort. But if it was so simple, why hadn't he shared the notebooks full of letters when I'd first started asking questions? Why had he kept them a secret in the first place?

"Who are you?" I whispered looking down at the letters. "Who *were* you?"

Had his experiences in the Navy shaped who he came home to be, even years later, as a husband and a father? Or was I just overthinking this, reading something into it that wasn't there? I'd had a happy childhood; I had no complaints. So why was I questioning everything now?

Wishing I could just pull out a reference book on Murray William Fisher, I came up with the next best thing. Perhaps if I made a list of what I knew about my father, something would shake loose, some revelation. Maybe I knew something but didn't realize it. That was possible, wasn't it?

"OK," I said. "What do you know about your dad?"

I grabbed my son's spiral notebook from the coffee table and tore out a page. "What I Know," I wrote at the top. I listed everything I knew about my father: where he was born, where he worked, how many siblings he had, how many children and grandchildren. I added his likes and dislikes. When I couldn't think of anything more, I'd only filled one page.

I glanced out the window and then back at the page. Everything on the list was so general, so generic. I read each item again, trying to expand on them, but couldn't. How could I be my father's daughter and know so little about him?

"This is nothing," I said frustrated.

I wadded the paper into a tight ball and threw it across the room. Then I sat puzzled by my own action, my own words. I was angry at myself for not knowing more about my father. But why was this affecting me so? Before he gave me the letters, I was satisfied with what I knew about my dad; I thought I knew everything there was to know. I shook my head and then picked up the paper and flattened it out. I read it aloud.

"This can't be all there is to you, Dad," I said quietly. "There's something more. I know there is."

We are all molded by our life experiences. Being sent off to war was one of those experiences for my father. But by all accounts he was one of the lucky ones who never saw any action. He'd been on ships and submarines but not in battle. In fact, after its bombing in 1941, Pearl Harbor was probably one of the safest places to be. And he'd spent the whole war there. It was just a two-year span of his life—nothing more. They were tumultuous times, yes, but he was protected, doing his work in an office. Over the last few years, I'd heard him say many times, "I wasn't *in* the war. The guys who were in hand-to-hand combat, they are the ones who were *in the war.*"

Turning off the light, I stood at the picture window. I looked past my birdfeeders, silhouetted in shadow, and stared at a dark place in the road. I gave my eyes time to adjust but I knew it wouldn't matter. That one place, too far from the streetlights on either side, remained dark. I shook my head.

"I wish something could be done about that," I whispered. "It's just too dark."

Feb 1, 1945

Dear Folks,

Well, I'm just about alone again now. All the rest of boys went out today except Jonesy (our ex section leader at Farragut). He was up to the Navy hospital getting a check-up on his back so guess he won't go for a little while.

Feel pretty lost today. Our school course just fizzled out. All the boys drafted out so guess it just ends. Was supposed to last until Saturday anyway. From now on guess I'll just loaf around twenty-four hours a day until I get my glasses.

I'm going to take a traffic management course thru the educational institute. That should help me later, when I go back to working for the railroad. It costs just two bucks at the start and you can take all the courses you want from then on for nothing as long as you keep your grades up, and hand in at least a lesson a month. Haven't any books or anything yet. I'll send my money order down to the office today and should get started in a few days. If I don't go to school I think I'll work out a school schedule of my own to pass the time away.

The only other railroad man that was here left yesterday. The whole thing makes me feel rather low. Was next to being home having anyone around that went thru radio school with me. It's a small world tho. I ran into one of the Farragut teachers this morning and had quite a gab session with him.

Didn't get any mail today on top of everything else. Mail at mail call always fixes up any boring long day. Maybe I'll have some tonite tho.

Be sure and rush along that foto album if you haven't already done so.

By the way, did you ever get those pictures of the Fiat and Cord developed? Rush them too. But above all—Write. Love, Murray

Feb 2, 1945

Dear Folks,

The tone of these letters should be changing about now. Got another from you today. And dated the 27th too. They're starting to come to my new address at last. That's pretty good service I'd say. Let me know how long mine take in getting there. Sure makes a guy feel like licking the world when letters come regularly.

Everyone is gone but Jonesy and myself now. We have a tent to ourselves now. We tell everyone that wants in that it leaks like a sieve when it rains (only it doesn't rain).

Keep all the letters coming this way you can, even if you have to resort to carbons. They mean absolutely everything. We watch the clock like on a monotonous job, waiting impatiently for time for mail call.

Say Gerry, when you write you can spend the entire time telling me about the latest on the Fiat. I enjoy that as much as anything. If possible, let me have some other pictures of you guys and the Fiat. I would especially like to see those new seats when they are installed. Be sure they slope back rather than remain level. You said you were thinking about covering them with Indian design blankets. I'd think they would sail away awfully easy and be hard to clean. Why not get some good fiber seat covers, something like I had in the '39 Buick and cut them down to fit? That way you could wash them at any time too. Of course I guess you could always cover any material you put on with these covers if you wanted to. Tell me all about it. I've heard from Iris [sister] just once so far but then that's about all the time she's had.

Well Dad, as long as Gerry is busy working on junior, why don't you limber his skis up for him. At least it would keep you off of street corners.

Days are kind of long with no school, no work, no nothing—Jonesy and I just sit around and gab about our families and friends and home. Then we look over each other's pictures again to see if we missed anything. Rush the album—we're running out of something to do.

Better go eat. Write. Love, Murray

I closed the notebook as sadness washed over me. My dad was hurting. He was lonely. Although the events took place long ago, his letters made them feel more immediate. His words transcended decades.

I thought back to the only time of true loneliness in my own life. It was a childhood memory. The summer after I turned nine, I went to Girl Scout camp with my best friend Kim. When she became sick with strep throat, her parents were called and quickly came to pick her up from our mountain cabin. I wandered around aimlessly, trying to fit in with the girls who'd already formed close friendships. I was miserable and I wanted to go home. In fact, I was so lonely that I faked strep throat, even gargling with Listerine for the nurse, several times a day. And it worked. My parents were called and I got to go back to the love and comfort of my family. And they never knew the truth about why I came home.

But reading my father's letters, I realized I'd never known loneliness, not really. On the base, two thousand miles from home, he wanted mail so badly that he would settle for carbon copies. He just wanted something from home. He wanted to look at the date at the top of the letter and know that someone had been thinking of him on that day. He imagined them sitting down at a place he could picture in his mind, perhaps the kitchen table or a desk by the bedroom window. His mother or father had taken a pen from the holder he'd touched just a few weeks before. And they'd taken the letter to the post office, just as he himself had done so many times.

He wanted news from home. He wanted to know about his brother's car and his mother's garden. He and his comrade, a friend due to circumstances, even read each other's letters after they'd memorized every line of their own. That sort of loneliness is profound.

As I sat on my comfortable sofa, knees drawn up to my chest, I held the fragile letter in my hand. Then a solution came to mind, a way to help him. "I should go get some stationery and my purple pen. I'll write him a quick letter and send him photographs of the kids. That will cheer him up."

I shook my head, unbelieving. How could I think such a crazy thought? More than fifty years had passed since he wrote those letters, and yet, for a fleeting moment I had a solution.

The door opened wide, I let myself imagine what it would

be like, if only I'd been his daughter then. Perhaps I'd start a letter-writing campaign. I would sit my sons and daughter down and explain to them how lonely Grandpa is.

Danielle is sixteen. She'll want to make her own card, writing encouraging words with colored markers. She'll attach stickers and draw hearts and swirls around the edges. Then before sealing the envelope, she'll sprinkle glitter inside.

Micah is twelve. He'll feel badly for Grandpa. He'll want to do something, but won't be sure how to go about it. He'll go with me to pick out a card. After analyzing each one, he'll choose the one that is the most meaningful. Then he'll ask me to tell him what to write. I'll give him several ideas and he'll write carefully.

Caleb is seven. I'll have a hard time getting him to sit still long enough to listen. But once he does, he'll begin by grabbing a piece of copy paper from the printer. He'll tell Grandpa about his soccer game and the goal he scored. He'll write quickly not worrying about spelling. Then he'll draw a quick picture: he's smiling and one leg is raised kicking the ball, scoring the goal. Then he'll hand me the letter as he runs out the door.

I smile imagining it all. And then I feel silly for entertaining such a thought.

My father had been lonely and homesick during the war. But the war was long past.

"If only I'd known him then," I tell myself. "I would have been the kind of daughter who was there for him. I would have. I would. But now?"

Now there is nothing to do. It was over, and I couldn't be there for him.

CHAPTER FIVE

Tell Me a Word

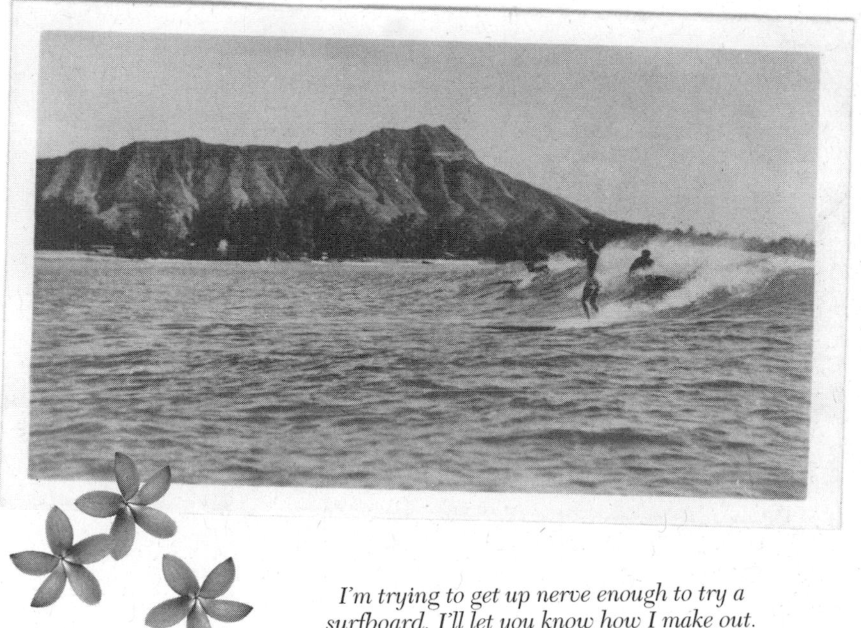

I'm trying to get up nerve enough to try a surfboard. I'll let you know how I make out.
—February 9, 1945

"You're going to do what?" my husband asked.

"Transcribe the letters," I said.

"You're going to type them all?"

"Well…yes," I replied.

"Why?" he asked. But he continued without letting me answer. "Karen, do you realize how much time that would take? We're already too busy and now you want to add something like this?"

"You've seen the letters," I said. "Dad's handwriting is hard to read. It's tiny and runs together. And the paper used back then is so thin and fragile."

But I knew he was right. My life was full and I was already chronically tired. I worked part time teaching children with disabilities at the local elementary school. In the afternoons, cooking, cleaning, shopping, and other chores filled my time. After school and evenings were spent chauffeuring the kids from one activity to another: soccer practice, music lessons, and school events. Somewhere amidst our tight schedule, we managed to eat dinner and supervise homework. Then it was bath time, story time, and bedtime. And the next morning the organized chaos began all over again.

Yet I couldn't shake the feeling that it needed to be done.

"I just want the kids to each have their own copy of my dad's letters," I said, trying to come up with an answer for what even I didn't understand.

"Then go down to Staples and make copies," he said.

That certainly made sense. But, I thought, maybe this wasn't about what *makes sense*. This was something that just felt right to me. There weren't any words to explain it, especially to my practical husband. So I gave up trying and decided to find my own time to work on them.

Each night after everyone was in bed, I sat alone with the letters, typing them into my word processor. When there was something I didn't understand, I wrote myself a note on whatever was handy—a scrap of paper, the back of an envelope, a receipt from the grocery store. A few weeks passed before I came up with a better way to keep track of my questions: simply setting the font to bold and writing the questions right into the text.

I stopped by my parents' house after work one day. Walking up the brick steps, I used the secret knock my father taught me when I was still in pigtails: four knocks, then a pause, and then two knocks.

It had always been our secret knock, but I'd only recently learned what it meant. My husband and I had just bought a fixer-upper near my parents' house, so Dad began visiting more often. He enjoyed riding over on his Segway, a stand-up scooter, to visit with his grandchildren or help with our latest home-improvement project. Each visit started with the same knock. So one day I asked him about it.

"Dad," I said, "as long as I can remember, we've used the same knock."

"Well, you know what it means, don't you?" he asked.

I shook my head.

"It's Morse code," he said.

"One, two, three, four...one, two," he said. "H...I." His fingers quickly tapped the air as he spoke. "It means 'hi' in Morse."

"I didn't know that," I said. "All this time, I just thought it was our secret knock."

He laughed.

With that fresh memory swirling in my mind, I let myself in my parents' house with a small smile on my face. I found my father sitting in his favorite recliner, watching TV.

"Hi, Dad," I said.

"Hi, yourself," he answered.

He searched the cluttered table next to him. Under magazines, books, and mail, he found the remote control and pressed mute. We talked for a few minutes about the weather and the book he was reading. I wanted to bring up the letters, but I didn't know how. Phone calls and visits to my parents' house usually consisted of a little small talk with Dad quickly followed by me asking for my mom. I was suddenly acutely aware that I really didn't talk to my dad all that much. I wanted to say, "Dad, tell me about the war." But the words hid.

"I've been reading your letters," I started.

"You have?" he asked.

"Yeah. They're pretty interesting," I said.

"Well I didn't think anyone would want to read those old things."

There was a barely noticeable lilt to his voice. Encouraged, I continued. "So when did Grandma give them to you?" I asked clumsily.

"I don't remember," he said. "Maybe a few years after I got home. I don't know."

"Did you know she had them before that? I mean did you know she saved them?" I asked.

"No," he replied. "I don't know. I just don't remember." There was frustration in his voice. "I just can't help you with this stuff. I don't remember anything. It was too long ago."

For most people his age, maybe this would be true. Fifty years is a long time to remember such details. But not for my father, who'd always had a meticulous memory. I knew better than that. Still, he'd given me the letters and even seemed pleased I was reading them.

He un-muted the television before I could ask another question. "This channel has some good old movies. This one is about..."

He went on to tell me all about the movie. I watched the screen as if *I* were muted. I tried to concentrate on it, to come up with a question to ask just to show an interest. But all I could think was, "How am I ever going to get him to talk to me?"

I'd come over hoping to have a conversation with him. I wanted to sit down and just talk, casually like I did with my girlfriends. I wanted to know what he thought and how he felt.

When I was growing up and even into adulthood, I had always talked to my dad and he had talked to me, but we never *really* had a conversation. And now, after almost forty years, we didn't know how to talk to each other. We only knew how to talk *at* each other. We knew how to wait politely for the other to finish talking. Eye contact was sparse and infrequent—we looked down, or around, or out the window.

We'd communicated this way all of my life. And now, when it mattered, it seemed too late to learn a new way.

I waited for a commercial. He always muted the sound on commercials. But this time he didn't. I watched more of the movie and another set of commercials. My father had been hard of hearing all of my life, so when the television volume was on, it was impossible to hold a conversation. He kept the sound on through another set of commercials.

He had no intention of talking to me.

Feb 9, 1945

Dear Folks,

I didn't have room in last letter to answer all your questions. No letters today so may get caught up.

We just about bought a radio a little while ago. They are hard to get and easy to get rid of. Someone beat us to it tho. You can always get rid of them in 5 minutes by putting up a notice on the bulletin board. And you don't need to take a loss either.

We have all the main radio programs and have a lot of military band and Hawaiian music instead of the soap operas in the states.

I'm trying to get up nerve enough to try a surfboard. I'll let you know how I make out. It looks easy but they say it's tricky.

Oh yes, Dad, they have Fiats and Cords here. I've seen two Cords and one Fiat. There are all makes and models of cars here. About the only difference is that the majority of them have all leather upholstery. Don't know just why.

When we went to see "The Mikado" last night, we went through the best part of town. I'd never been there before. Very nice houses and a Sears store is located way out on the edge of town. It's a super-modern, one-story building as are most of the large stores in town. We saw the university campus too. It was really nice—lots of grass, which was something neat to see. Camp is all just dirt and tents.

Well, guess you know by now what my deal is here. Waiting for glasses now. The doc seemed quite upset about my eyes so maybe something cooking. If so, I would probably get a restricted or limited service rating and be assigned to a shore base. Otherwise could be on ship or an advanced base. Will be a while yet before anything happens tho.

The place is about deserted now. You'll just have to guess why and read the papers.

Days are sure long—you'd probably all like to trade with me. Get up around 715, eat breakfast 730 just across the street. Muster at 750. Then nothing until noon. Eat around noon or one and nothing until 530 p.m. Have supper then. Go to a show at seven and back at nine or so—lights out at ten. Mail call at noon and five p.m.

A very invigorating existence. Spend rest of time browsing around ships service, drinking Nesbit orange pop, visiting tent library and reading and writing letters. I may have to resort to building model airplanes soon.

Better get a letter off to Iris. Think I've written an average of almost three a day in past month. I've been on the island just a month now. Write. Love, Murray

As I read through more of his letters, I realized I was looking for something, a clue perhaps. But a clue to what? A clue to why he'd kept the letters a secret? That was part of it. But there was more. I had the unmistakable feeling that I'd missed something. When I read the line in his letter that said, "The place is deserted now. You'll just have to guess why and read the papers," something quickened in me. And something else bothered me.

Dad has a favorite game that says a lot about his memory for detail. He likes to challenge me, "Say a word, any word, and I'll tell you a story about it." Then I say some random word like, "horse" or "red" or "sidewalk." He thinks for just a moment and then recalls some story, some obscure parable from his past. He recalls details that anyone else would never have committed to memory in the first place. So why couldn't he answer any of the questions I asked him?

It didn't fit with what I knew about him. He could read a complicated, technical book and then use the information years later, from memory, to design or fix something. Our family had long thought he had a photographic memory, though he was adamant that he didn't.

Then I remembered something important: his memory for detail was never more obvious than when he wrote an email.

My father had been online since the Internet first came to town. In fact, he is proud to share that he was one of the first in Walla Walla to have it. When I finally jumped on the Internet bandwagon, I realized what a prolific writer he was. The whole family gives him a hard time about his extremely long emails. "Ask me what time it is," he jokes, "and I'll tell you how to build a watch." And it's true. If I emailed, casually asking how lunch was, he'd reply with every detail: who he went with, where they ate, what they ate, how it tasted, and what the conversation entailed.

It was this attention to detail that gave me an idea: perhaps if I put my questions to him in an email, he would answer me, without the awkwardness we both seemed to feel when we talked in person.

Though I tried to save working on the letters for nighttime, I couldn't wait to try this. After supper, I propped my laptop on my knees, opened to the letters I'd typed so far. I minimized the page to half the size of the screen and then opened my email and transferred the bolded questions. I numbered each one and left space for him to answer. I hit send and butterflies invaded my stomach.

I wondered if he'd even respond. My predictable father had become unpredictable to me. He'd never failed to answer an email promptly in the past. But after my failure to get him to answer the simplest of questions, I wasn't sure of anything anymore. I'd just have to wait and see.

The next day, I received a three-page response. He answered each question in the blank space I had left. And just as I'd predicted, he answered in detail.

The first question was about his glasses.

"In your letters, you always seem to be getting your glasses fixed. Could you tell me about your glasses?"

He told the story, starting when he was a little boy.

Dad was eight years old when, one day, as he was walking with his dad, he commented on the two cows in the pasture.

"Two cows?" My grandpa laughed.

Dad repeated his observation.

"There aren't two cows," Grandpa said. "There is only one."

That is how my father found out that it wasn't normal to see everything in duplicate. From then on he wore thick glasses, and unlike others his age, he was happy to wear them.

The glasses issued to him by the United States Navy were flimsy, the lenses tended to pop out easily, and his prescription was not a standard one, so getting it right was a perennial problem.

I scrolled down the page, browsing the responses to each question. One…two…three…I smiled when I saw the answers and the detail to each. Then I got to the last question, number four.

"In your letter dated February 9, 1945, you say, *The place is about deserted now. You'll just have to guess why and read the papers.* Do you remember what you were talking about?"

The space below it was blank. Maybe he didn't notice it, I thought. But before the thought was even complete, I knew it was unlikely. My dad didn't miss things like that.

Perhaps he'd answer it later. I checked my email periodically over the next few days. Still no answer.

Finally convinced that an answer was not forthcoming, I printed off a copy of the email, grabbed the notebook, and drove over to my parents' house. I didn't know what to expect but I knew I had to try.

When I pulled into the driveway, the double garage door was up and he was hammering away at something in the shop inside.

"Hi, Dad," I said coming up behind him.

"Well, hello," he said smiling. "What're you doing here?"

He glanced at the paper in my hand.

"The email," I said cautiously. "There was one more question. You probably didn't see it."

"Hmm," he said.

He went back to hammering.

I stood behind him, waiting. Maybe he just needed to finish what he was working on. I waited some more. He didn't look back, not even a glance over his shoulder. As the noise continued, I slowly came to the realization that he wasn't going to respond to me. So I slowly turned and went inside the house.

Mom greeted me at the door.

"You look nice," I said.

Though in her seventies, she always had someplace to go, a meeting, a church group, or lunch with friends.

"Thank you," she said. "What do you think of the necklace with this?" Mom always dressed stylishly in slacks, colorful blouses, and coordinating jackets. "Does it look OK?" she asked.

"It looks great," I said.

"Oh, good. I'm meeting a friend at the church in an hour," she said.

She went into the other room and returned with a box of chocolates. She opened the box and set it on the coffee table in front of me and then sat on the sofa with her back to the picture window. The sun made her silver hair sparkle like glitter.

"I've been reading Dad's letters," I said. "And I emailed him some questions."

"I heard," she said, pursing her lips. "He printed them off to show me."

"Did he tell you he didn't answer all the questions?" I asked.

"No," she replied. There was no surprise in her voice.

"Listen to this," I said.

I glanced at the front door before reading from the letter dated February 9, 1945.

Well, guess you know by now what my deal is here, I read.

"And then this," I added. *The place is about deserted now. You'll just have to guess why and read the papers.*

I looked at her and squinted.

"I asked him what he meant when he wrote that," I said. "He answered all the other questions, but not this one."

"Well, he's in the garage, ask him," she said.

"I know," I responded, looking over the chocolates. "I tried to ask him but I don't think he wants to answer. He was hammering away at something."

A little bit later, Dad walked through the living room to the kitchen without looking at me. I heard the water running as he washed his hands. When he returned, he sat down in the recliner and set his Bowfin submarine cap on the end table next to him. He smoothed his hair to one side.

"Why are you doing this?" he asked.

"I don't know, Dad. All I *do* know is that these letters are a gift, and I want to understand what's in them. I just want to know more. I can't explain it."

"It was Iwo Jima," he said abruptly. "That letter I wrote must have been referring to Iwo Jima. It was in all the newspapers. So many guys were sent out that the base was pretty much deserted. I couldn't talk about it in my letters because of the censors, but I knew my folks would be reading about it in the newspaper back home."

"What exactly was Iwo Jima?" I asked.

"Well, you know," he began, "Iwo Jima was just a tiny island. It was only about five miles long and maybe two miles across. Admiral Nimitz wanted the island for a place to refuel our B-29s. You've probably seen the photograph of the marines raising the flag on Iwo."

I nodded.

"That became the most famous photograph of WWII," he explained.

As he started to talk, I remembered the notebook and pen I'd brought. They were in my purse on the floor, but I was afraid he'd stop talking if I looked away, even for a moment. So I kept my eyes on him. He stared at the blank television screen as he spoke, but it felt like he was staring at *me*. I didn't move.

"So the flag was raised after they'd overtaken the island?" I asked.

He laughed, a sparkle in his eyes.

"The thought was that it would only take a few days to take the island from the Japs," he said. "That's what we called them back then: Japs. Anyway, our guys went in and strafed the beaches."

"Strafed?" I asked.

"Oh, you don't know what strafing is, do you? I suppose you wouldn't. Strafing was when you sent up these small planes and they flew in low, shooting up the beaches. We…they…could see that sand and dirt and dust in a cloud over the beach. Every grain of sand was turned over several times. Everyone thought the Japs were hiding by burying themselves in the sand. And I suppose a few were. But for the most part, I don't think it helped at all. The Japs had an elaborate tunnel system on that island. They were in caves that were connected by tunnels all through it.

"So, back to the flag. It was raised on Mount Suribachi four days after the initial landing. We…they…could see it from the water. But it took a total of thirty-five days I think, before we had taken the whole island."

He sat back in his chair and looked out the window.

"So that's the story," he said.

My mind was whirling. Had he misspoken when he said "we"? Or was there something more to it? Clearly, he was done talking. He was quiet now, as if in deep thought. Time passed as we sat silently. There was something about his demeanor that held an invisible hand up, refusing to let me pursue it.

"Are you going to Caleb's soccer game?" I finally asked.

He was quiet.

"Dad?" I asked.

"What?"

"Caleb's game?" I asked again.

"Oh, yes. We'll be there. What time does it start?"

CHAPTER SIX

Two Questions, One Answer

Another day. Nothing new.
Saw a very good U.S.O. show last night.
—February 15, 1945

Ric had already left for work when the kids piled into my car for the ride to school. I tossed my purse and book bag into the backseat and buckled in. I had a trick to be sure the kids buckled in quickly too: I wouldn't start the car until I heard three clicks. Click, click, click.

I turned the key. Nothing happened. I turned it again. Nothing. There was no sound, no turning over, just silence. I looked at my watch. My carefully timed morning had just taken a huge hit.

"Everybody out," I said.

"But, Mom," Danielle said, "I'm supposed to meet Casey before school."

"I can't be late," Micah joined in.

Caleb was already out and jumping up and down beside the car.

I groaned loudly as I bolted up the steps and back inside. Not only did I need a ride, I also needed somebody to give all my kids a ride. That was a lot to ask of anybody. And the only people I'd feel comfortable asking were my mom and dad.

I picked up the phone and dialed my parents, quickly explaining the situation to Dad. Mom had left for a prayer group, but Dad quickly agreed. While he was on his way, I phoned the school where I worked to let them know I'd be a few minutes late.

We all got into Grandpa's car and I wrote excuses for each of them on the way to their schools. After the kids were delivered, he drove me to *my* school.

As he pulled up in front, I said good-bye and made him promise to pick me up right after my part-time teaching job ended at noon. I felt like a little kid again, getting dropped off by my daddy.

"Are you hungry?" Dad asked when he picked me up.

"Yeah. I guess," I said.

"Me too. How about lunch?" he asked.

He drove us to Stone Soup, a little soup and sandwich shop. Inside, it was crowded with downtown business people, the line stretching from the counter to the door. Behind the counter, employees in white aprons made sandwiches and ladled soup from large pots. The menu was written on a large chalkboard. Enchilada soup was the Wednesday special. I ordered a cup and Dad ordered a bowl. I pulled out my checkbook but he insisted on paying. I poured ice water into Styrofoam cups while he found us a seat at one of the little round tables.

My father had read tons of books on every aspect of the war over the years, and I'd been reading about Iwo Jima, so now I had a little background information. Unlike the more personal questions, the general ones would often launch him into lengthy and detailed answers—though, he never offered information on his own. So, I asked a few questions about Iwo

Jima. But his answers were uncharacteristically short. Then, to my surprise, he asked a question of his own.

"Why do you suppose my mother kept the letters?" he asked.

I shrugged. I hadn't thought about it.

"I don't know," I said.

"I guess I'll never know," he said as he finished his soup.

"Dad?" I asked. "Would it be OK with you if I put your letters in archive-safe sleeves? They're plastic and have holes punched so I could put them in binders."

I looked down and dipped the spoon past the crunchy strips of tortillas on top.

"I don't care," he said. "I mean, I don't know. I don't want you to go to any trouble or anything."

"It's no trouble," I explained. "Actually, it would be easier. The paper is so thin and I've been researching on the Internet. I found out that it's not good to handle the actual letters over and over. I also talked with our school librarian. She said the same thing. In fact, I took the notebooks to school and showed her. You should have seen the look on her face. She was so excited that I was transcribing them."

"Transcribing?" he asked. "You're transcribing them?"

I'd forgotten to tell him. It had just come about so naturally, that it didn't feel like I really made the decision at all. It was just another tentative step on this journey we'd started together. I looked at him, hoping to read his reaction. We were right across from each other, no more than twelve inches away. He glanced up from his soup a few times, but his expression never changed.

"Yeah," I said. "I'm transcribing them."

"You mean you're typing every letter?" he asked, putting down his spoon.

"Yeah," I answered.
"Why?" he asked in the same tone I'd heard months earlier.
"I don't know," I said.

Feb 14, 1945

Dear Folks,

Yesterday, I decided early to get my traffic course application signed. Then got permission to go to Honolulu to the main offices to get the actual course and get started. Got all that done by 1 pm and then went out to Waikiki to a show, "None But the Lonely Heart." Not bad. Ate all the ice cream in every form I could get my hands on and caught a bus back to landing and by boat to camp again.

As for the course, they gave me the whole works all at once. In case I move around I'll have it all with me that way. It consists of 27 books about like my radio course and three big folding maps with Freight Classification Territory and various railroads in U.S. and Canada marked. The course seems to be quite thorough. It covers freight tariffs, rail and water rates, and routes tracing and expediting—air express and parcel post regulation to mention a few. Looks very interesting especially since I already have a kind of haphazard knowledge of a lot of it. In this course it's all catalogued right so it's kind of a bridge toward getting my present knowledge and learning more later, together.

As I finish a few lessons I'm going to send the books home so you can look them over. I'm going to figure out a plan now to study when it's cool in the morning so I can get the most done. Jonesy is going to take a course in accounting while he is here so we've decided to run a regular classroom schedule. Just in the morning tho. Afternoons get too hot to work.

I've gone about a week with no mail again. Something's sure wrong with my mail—Jonesy hardly misses a day. I'm going to start tracking it down if don't get any tomorrow. Let me know how mine is getting to you—if it skips a few days and arrives in bunches or they come about the same length of time all along.

Nothing new in any line, still loafing.

Write soon. Love, Murray

Feb 15, 1945

Dear Folks,

Another day. Nothing new. Saw a very good U.S.O. show last night…All soldier cast. Also, they opened our new outdoor theatre. It's called, Phillips Theatre. It's just a few steps from our tent. The other one was several blocks.

This camp isn't really the nicest in the world. Not a blade of grass and not a tree. Just lots of dirt and very hot sun. Believe 'tis kind of an existence would get monotonous after the first few months.

Got a flock of magazines yesterday. Most of them almost up to date too. A lot of them we've been getting are quite old. Usually December issues.

Studied a third of the way thru my first lesson. Have 27 lessons. So far it is very simple and easy to understand.

Well Jonesy is still with me. I told you he was having trouble with his back. He had it checked by the local doctor who then sent him up to the hospital on the island for a complete check up and x-ray. The x-ray showed it perfectly normal as far as bone structure is concerned. However it seems there can be plenty wrong with a back that's not discernable by the naked eye nor by x-ray. For example your trouble Dad, the sacroiliac joint can cause trouble without anything at all being visible. That seems to be Jonesy's trouble. He was in an auto accident about same as mine and wrenched his back. Everyone says keep after them if your back really bothers you as they can't really do much with it. Jonesy is taking some pills and two treatments a day but doc admits it isn't going to ever do any real good except to relieve it for a while. You know he's here just like me on "borrowed time." Last time doc gave him 3 days more of heat treatments. And then going to check him again. Tomorrow is the check-up day—then will know. It's a cinch they won't send him out like he is. The hospital recommended limited services—which means a desk job in the states. Anyway he'll know tomorrow then I'm going to work. About mail time—I'll get this in and see if I've got some for a change.

Write. Love, Murray

I sat at my dining table and opened the notebook. Taking the first letter out, I carefully slid it into the sleeve and then put it in the new notebook I'd just bought. When the first of the worn notebooks was empty, I closed it and saw something I hadn't noticed before. The initials R.J.F. were printed in slanted letters in one corner of the notebook. Raymond James Fisher was my dad's little brother. Slightly above the initials was '41. I traced it with my finger. Then the answer came to me, an answer to the question my father had asked over tortilla soup.

"Because she didn't know," I said aloud. "She didn't know if her boy would return from the war."

I gently turned the pages. I was taken back in time to a grandmother I'd never met, a mother who feared for her son. That's why she had saved the letters. They were a part of him. She'd used an old two-ring notebook that my uncle had used in high school. And every time she got a letter in the mail, she'd put it in the notebook. It was proof that her beloved son, more than two thousand miles away, was still alive. She saved them because the next correspondence she received could be a telegram that started with the words "We regret to inform you..." Every letter could be the last. And when the last letter she received from him was followed by her son stepping off the train, she didn't need them anymore. She had her son. She put the letters away—until one day she gave them back to him.

When I finished transferring the letters to the archive-safe sleeves, I had filled four black notebooks and gone through four one hundred-packs of sleeves. My father had written more than four hundred pages of letters to his folks during the war. What a treasure they must have been to them, but especially to his mother.

He had asked me, "Why are you doing this?" and I couldn't answer. But slowly an answer was forming. I was finishing what my grandmother had started. Something was driving me to transcribe the letters. I thought it was for my children. And it was, but there was something more.

CHAPTER SEVEN

Wednesdays with Murray

Went to show…at the end of the reel there's a blackout while the projectionist changes reels. And it always happens at the critical instances in the movie.—February 15, 1945

That first Wednesday soon became a routine. Dad and I continued to eat lunch together every week for the remainder of the school year. But as summer approached and temperatures soared into the nineties, we decided that soup no longer sounded very good. Dad had heard that a local diner, Mr. Ed's, served his all-time favorite: eggs Benedict. So we started going there for breakfast. By the time colder weather came, we had become comfortable in our new routine.

I continued to read the letters, but I saved my questions for our weekly time together. Each Wednesday, I took out a list of questions and then gently fit them between bites of eggs Benedict and crispy hash browns. Sometimes, the answers flowed easily. But more often than not, they didn't. I walked a fine line that was now far too familiar. His responses to the questions were completely unpredictable. Questions that I thought might upset him didn't. Questions I didn't think would upset him did. It seemed to be less about the subject matter and more about the memory a word or thought triggered.

Between Wednesdays, I emailed questions to him; sometimes he responded, sometimes he didn't. The whole system wasn't very efficient and didn't fit with my methodical personality. Still, my late night transcribing had finally added up to one notebook of letters completed and three to go. I went to bed each night with my neck aching and my vision blurry. It was a laborious task, trying to read his tiny handwriting, gleaning information from the letters and from him, and then attempting to form a mental timeline and keep up with the questions that popped into my head relentlessly. And then there was the military jargon and the 1940s language that I didn't understand.

My husband had been right when he worried this would take a lot of time. Perhaps he knew me better than I knew myself. He knew I couldn't simply type the letters and leave it at that. I had to understand. *One letter at a time*, I kept telling myself. And that's how it went.

I sat on my bed, pillows propped behind me and comforter pulled over my legs. I switched on the heating blanket and balanced my laptop on knees. My kitty jumped on the bed, circling a few times before curling up on my feet. I opened the word processor to the letters I'd transcribed so far. I'd finished one notebook of the original letters, one hundred pages. But as I scrolled down, I realized I wasn't really done with them. There were many places in his letters where I couldn't decipher his writing. Instead of stopping when I came to a place like that, I'd moved on. But now, looking at it, I hated all those blank spaces on the page.

I dialed Dad's number.

"Dad," I said, "I need to come over tomorrow."

"Come on over anytime," he said.

"You might want to hear *why* before you agree to this," I said.

"Well, as long as I don't have to do any work," he joked.

"*Actually*," I teased, and then added, "it is a bit of work I need from you. But I'll do most of it."

I arrived the next day with my laptop and one of the notebooks.

"OK, Dad," I said. "Let's get started."

"I don't like the look of this," he said. "This definitely looks like work."

I handed him the notebook of his letters. He looked at me as if I'd just put a snake in his lap. But I pretended not to notice. I opened my computer and scrolled down, hoping this would work.

"Let me explain how I've been doing this," I said. "Your handwriting is sometimes hard to read. So when I was typing and I came to a word or phrase I couldn't read, I left a long line of dashes."

I turned the laptop around and showed him.

"Now all I have to do is go back, delete the dashes, and fill in the blanks," I said. "And that's where you come in."

"I don't think I can help you there." He laughed. "I can't read my own handwriting, you know."

"Well, we can at least try, right?" I asked.

"I guess," he replied.

"OK," I said. "Turn to the letter dated January 22, 1945."

"Got it," he said.

"OK. Now go to the first sentence of the last paragraph," I said.

And so it went for the next hour. Most of the time Dad was able to fill in the unknown words easily. But sometimes it was more difficult and I'd kneel next to his chair as we read and reread the sentence, looking carefully at each letter, comparing it to others, or using the context of the sentence to figure it out.

"You know why these are so hard to read?" he asked. "I wrote whenever I could and that was usually late at night in my bunk, with very little light."

"Hmm," I said. "That's not how I pictured it. I pictured you at a desk or something."

"Actually, I rarely sat at a desk or table to write, until I started working in an office. But that was later in the war. Is there a place where my letters change from being handwritten to being typed?" he asked.

"Yes, there is. And your typing is a lot easier to read than your handwriting," I teased.

We finished several letters that first day. And in the coming weeks, I found it was something I could fit between the rest of my life—between running errands and paying bills, or between grocery shopping and cleaning the house, an hour here and an hour there. It was a slow process. So many letters had accumulated that, when I had the time, I wanted to just barrel on through. Dad didn't have the same sense of urgency. In fact, he usually ended our session before I was ready. He was always nice about it. In fact, he simply threw out hints: his back hurt, he had an errand to run, he wanted to take an afternoon nap. "Do you want to stop?" I'd ask. The answer was always yes.

I began to suspect there was something more to the often abrupt end to our time together. But regardless of the reason, when *he* was done, *we* were done.

Feb 15, 1945

Dear Folks,

Believe I wrote you once today but I have half an hour to kill before show time. Jonesy just checked with the doctor a few minutes ago and the doc took him right up to the local hospital for a few days observation. All of a sudden, just like that. It's just a few blocks from here on the same base so I'm going to take his mail to him and visit him now and then. He probably won't be there long.

I really stumbled on to something today. Probably of no importance now but you never can tell. Had mail-man check my mail-card at the main post office while he was over there yesterday. He says according to that, I was assigned to the office on another base as a communication specialist. Even showed what room I worked in and everything. He said he didn't change it because he thought I lived here and was working over there. Evidently when I was up for transfer a couple of weeks ago I was assigned to this other base. It's just the main office of this base I'm working at now. Over all of the other small bases around here—much closer to town and much nicer surroundings. They have every fourth day off and are usually there for a year or two years or even longer. A good deal. Don't have any idea what it will mean as far as getting a transfer when and if I leave my present location. Maybe that it's just held open for me when I get ready to go. Sure hope so. I wouldn't mind the place as long as I have to be in anyway.

Didn't do anything, as usual, today. Took a shower and shaved. I went to show and slept. The show, "To Have and Have Not" was very good. Most of the ones we see are a little old, but all of the best grade. We have two theatres—one is indoor and in one of the buildings that houses the communications school. All the buildings (with few exceptions) of any semi-permanent nature are of the Quonset hut type. You've probably seen 'em in shows. They are made of the corrugated tin in a big half-moon shape with inside made to fit the job they are to perform. Hospital, chapel, schools, living quarters and so forth. As I started to say about shows—this one here has just one projector. So at the end of the reel there's a blackout while the projectionist changes reels. And it always happens at the critical instances in the movie. Then at the other theatre which just opened—there's a show every night. It's in a huge fan shaped area with a big closed in stage and screen. Has just hardwood barracks with no benches with no backs for seats. That's all the officers have too, so we don't holler.

Very interesting, all this, huh, Mom? Say, if you should ever want to send anything this way—candy, cookies or anything at all put them in a good wood box or metal. Cardboard boxes aren't worth sending—they are wrecks when they get here.

Write. Love, Murray

A month and a half into his time on Oahu my father decided to find out why he wasn't getting his mail regularly. Everyone else seemed to. But Dad went days without a single letter and then got a bunch of them. So one day, he decided to hop in a jeep and go over to the post office. When an officer told him the address he had for my father, he was dumbfounded. The address was wrong.

Then the officer took him to the address. Inside the communications building was an office. My father's name was on the door. A desk was in there, with supplies and papers spread about as if he worked there every day. He didn't know just why, but it sent shivers down his spine. No one could explain it and my father didn't pursue it any further. As far as he knew, the office remained just as he'd seen it for the remainder of the war.

But years later he would reflect, "It was eerie. I didn't know what it meant. Maybe it was just a mistake. Maybe it wasn't."

CHAPTER EIGHT

By Design

Finished first day of school. It's just a refresher course in everything we had before, mostly just to pass the time I'd guess.—January 22, 1945

Dad and I had just finished editing for the day. I reached down, opened my backpack on the floor next to me, and slid my laptop into the padded compartment. Smaller compartments held other necessities: pens, pencils, and paper clips, as well as ibuprofen for the occasional headache. I took a yellow sticky note out and pressed it onto the plastic-encased letter we'd ended with and put the notebook into my backpack too. I stood up, stretching, and went to the kitchen.

"Do you want a glass of water?" I asked.

"No, thanks," he answered.

When I returned to the living room, Dad was rummaging through a plastic grocery bag. He pulled out a candy bar and then held the bag out to me.

"Choose one," he said. "They're much better for you than water."

Inside the bag were four or five different kinds of candy bars, twenty or so in all.

"Sale, huh?" I asked.

"Three for a dollar," he said. "Take several."

We sat back with our candy bars. He watched the muted television. I snuck glances at him.

"Did you have any friends during the war?" I asked.

As soon as I said it, I wished I hadn't. The words "friend" and "war" didn't sound right in the same sentence. But it was too late.

So I tried to explain. "Well, you know, is there anybody that you hung out with or became friends with on base?"

Silence.

When Mom stopped to chat on her way through the living room, it was an interruption we were both grateful for. We talked a little about her flower bulbs and the green beans cooking on the stove that smelled so good. But then a look came over her face and she said, "You two are busy. I'll leave you alone." And before I could say anything, she was gone, clinking around in the kitchen.

I wanted to bow out gracefully—if that was possible. But a vest of weights held me down. I couldn't just leave. Even though Mom had interrupted my question, I knew Dad wasn't easily distracted. I'd finished my candy bar, so I didn't even have that to focus my attention on. So I waited, trying to think of another subject to bring up.

"I did have one friend," he suddenly said. "I don't remember much about him. But his name was Mal."

Then, to my surprise, my father started to talk freely. His tone was matter-of-fact, even happy, as he spoke of his friend. He began on the day they met.

For those still on the base, there was a morning ritual. They went to an outdoor bulletin board to look for their name on the long list posted each day. Sailors on the list could expect to be in the next group to be shipped out into the battle. Every time my father checked the board, he saw different faces. But one day, he saw a young man who looked familiar.

My father ran his finger down the list of names, and then leaned against the side of the bulletin board.

"I can't believe it," Dad said.

"You too?" the man asked.

Dad glanced at him.

"Yeah," he answered. "Everyone else follows the same pattern. It's alphabetical. We're drafted out alphabetically, or we're supposed to be anyway."

The man nodded.

"I know," he said. "Then when it gets to your name, it's skipped. Am I right?"

Dad nodded, adding, "I just don't understand. I should have been drafted out several times by now."

"Well, hey, maybe they lost our records," the man joked, "and we'll just have to stay here in Hawaii for the remainder of the war."

"Wouldn't *that* be great?" Dad said.

They didn't know it then, but their meeting and that short conversation was just the beginning.

They went their separate ways assuming they'd never see each other again. The base was huge, and two servicemen could serve their entire tour of duty there and never see each other.

"We might as well have lived in different cities," my father recalled.

A few days after their meeting, a jeep parked in front of Dad's tent. The driver, an armed sailor, stood in the doorway to the tent.

"Fisher, Murray?" he inquired.

"That's me," my father answered.

The sailor then asked for my father to recite his ID number, which he did.

"You are to come with me," the sailor said.

My father sat in the passenger side as the driver zigzagged through the tent city, without speaking. My father's questions were met with stony silence. When he got to the destination, one of the many buildings on the base, the sailor told him to go inside and await further instructions.

Inside, another sailor was waiting for him. He led my father to a room. When he opened the door, there stood the young man from the bulletin board. A small group of men and an instructor had also assembled. They took their seats at a table, each as confused as the next. But then the officer in charge started to speak and things started to make sense.

All of the times their names had been skipped on drafts were not by mistake but by design. Each man at the table had been left on base while their comrades were sent out into the war for a very important reason.

My father and Mal would be part of a small and elite group. The team's mission: to copy and break a top-secret Japanese code transmitted in Katakana.

I could hardly believe what I was hearing. Such a simple question had led my father to share this new revelation. I dared not ask a question, for fear that I'd break the spell and never know what secrets he harbored.

When they'd met, both men wondered if there was a glitch in the system. Now their question was answered. There wasn't a glitch in the system at all. The system was working just fine. In radio school, months earlier, when the former FBI agent taught my father Katakana *just for fun*, plans had been set in motion.

As they sat in class that day, my father learned that unlike him, each of the other men, five in all, had been sent to code-breaking school. They were told that from now on everything they were told during these special sessions was top secret. They were not to reveal it to their tent mates or anyone else. They would be watched at all times to ensure they hadn't revealed anything. Their mail would be censored. They were not to talk about it in letters home, to family or friends. Even a hint would be reason for court martial.

At the end of the day, five separate vehicles took the men back to their tents. The driver was different from the one who'd brought him that morning. This time, my father didn't speak. He didn't ask any questions as the sailor drove in a roundabout way, finally dropping him at his tent.

As he lay on his bunk that night, he mentally went through all that had happened, beginning at Farragut where he'd learned the code. He hadn't been told any of the logistics of the mission: when, where, how. In a way, he was as much in the dark as he had been when the jeep pulled up that morning. But he liked code breaking. He liked copying code and he was glad he'd get to use what he'd learned. He went to bed that night wondering about what was to come.

The next morning, he was surprised when a military green

car pulled up in front of the tent at a different time than the day before. Again, a sailor asked for "Fisher, Murray." Again my father gave his ID number. He got into the car and the sailor took a different route, again, winding through the brick-red dirt roads.

If my father was expecting to arrive at the same building as the day before, he was mistaken. It was a different building. A different driver. A different vehicle. A different instructor. The only thing that remained the same was the group of men that gathered in the training room. At the end of the day, he was taken back to his barracks via a different route.

Several days in a row followed the same routine. The only thing that was routine about it was that someone would pick him up, take him someplace, and he would learn something then be taken back to his tent by someone. His chauffeurs were never the same. The vehicles he was picked up in changed. The instructors changed often, though a few returned a couple of times. The location changed each day. Some days the room was in a seemingly abandoned building. One day it might be an office; the next, it could be an equipment storage room.

As the days went by, something was changing in him. He'd been happy-go-lucky and even nonchalant about the war before, but now he was suspicious. He watched everyone around him. He held the secrets close, his mind reeling at even the most mundane of questions from his comrades.

The only thing the soldiers could count on staying the same was each other. Of the team of five, my father and Mal gravitated toward each other most. Mal was younger than my father, just nineteen years old, and Dad began to feel protective of him. But he also marveled at how brilliant Mal was; he was so young to be a part of this code-breaking team. They talked a little about their hometowns during short breaks, but they never revealed very much. Every part of the team seemed to be afraid of developing any kind of closeness with their team members. And yet, they had become like an estranged family reunited by a common goal. Each was the one constant in the other's life. At the end of the day, they were each sent their separate ways and didn't see each other on base at all. Looking back, my father wonders if that was by design, too.

Classes ranged from subjects like the technical aspects of radio communication to the technicalities of submarine submersion. But no instructor ever seemed to know what the other had taught. And even the students didn't know enough to piece it together. They were just given pieces to the puzzle. As hard as they tried, it seemed the pieces didn't fit the same puzzle at all.

One day, after a few weeks of the secretive classes, a sailor with sidearms came once again to my father's tent. He wove through the base, but this time the destination was different, very different: the base airport. There, a small airplane—barely big enough for its handful of passengers, which included my father and his new friend, Mal—awaited them. A short time later, they were on the island of Maui.

For weeks before, the base on Oahu had been alive with activity but then had turned eerily calm. With servicemen being sent out in large groups, the base was all but deserted. After all this time of waiting and wondering, he was standing with the small group of men on the island of Maui. What did it mean?

Like a dream or maybe a nightmare, he found himself beneath palm trees and in the bushes, learning things like how to slit the enemy's throat without him making a noise. This is what was called jungle warfare training. The men were shown an example and then practiced on each other.

"Come up behind him," the instructor said. "OK, now shove your forearm in his mouth and slit his throat with the other hand."

They practiced for hours, as their time on Maui would be short.

"Now, this is how to break a Jap's arm, rendering him defenseless," the instructor continued.

My father went along with the training. They all did.

When they weren't outdoors training, they were in the classroom, where they were taught Japanese. If they should be captured, hopefully these short lessons would come back to them, and they'd be able to understand what their captors were saying. After spending so much time on the base while others were sent out, the war was suddenly very real for my father.

Mal and my father were now part of a top-secret code-breaking team. Each person had a specific and crucial job to do. But without each other, the job couldn't be done at all. My father and Mal were both Katakana code specialists; they copied the code. The rest of the team consisted of the cryptanalyst, who deciphered the code; the technician, who kept the communications equipment working; and an officer who oversaw the whole operation.

After a few days on Maui, they were flown back to Oahu and told only that they would be leaving the island soon. They were ordered to start writing letters to their family. My father followed the orders, post-dating letter after letter, sealing and addressing the envelopes. But instead of mailing them, the letters were given to someone else who would send one every day or two while he was gone. His parents would never see a break in the frequent letters they were so used to getting and wouldn't suspect he was off the base.

The team was kept in the dark. No one knew where they were going. Would they be sent, as so many had, to the initial invasion of Iwo Jima?

The special classes continued on Oahu but took on a more sinister tone.

"What you will be doing is top secret," the instructor said one day. "We will have people watching you wherever you go. If you go to a restaurant, you can be assured we will have someone there watching you. If you are sitting at a bar, the guy next to you could be one of ours. If you talk, if you say anything about what you are doing, we will know about it."

The air in the classroom was already thick with fear, but what the sergeant said next brought a chill to the room.

"If you reveal anything about what you are doing, you will be sent to solitary for the remainder of the war. If what you revealed compromises security, you will be shot, without court-martial."

With fear and suspicion swirling around them, my father and Mal found comfort in being in each other's presence. The only people they could trust were each other. Anyone could be a spy. Anyone, of any class or rank, even a civilian, could be the one who was watching.

One day, they ran into each other outside of class. Though their friendship was one of few words, they decided to go off base to Nimitz Beach to relax a little. They sat on the beach, talking and watching the waves crash against the shore. When they got too hot, they swam way out in the surf, enjoying the warm water. Beyond the last waves, clear ocean water surrounded them as far as they could see in all directions. Treading water, my father asked Mal, "So do you think it would be safe to talk out here?"

"I don't think that would be a good idea," Mal said.

My father agreed.

And with that, the foundation of their friendship was set. It was a friendship that had its own protocol. Back at home in civilian life, he would have gabbed with friends about the ups and downs of the job, of family and leisure time activities. But now, he and Mal could talk of nothing in the past and nothing in the future. Their communication was stunted as each worried about where even a casual conversation might lead. It was easier to not talk at all than to censor each word.

Still, they were in this together. They knew the secrets they must keep. Their friendship grew despite being deprived of sunlight. Somehow it thrived without words. They signed a contract with their silence. It was a vow they would never break.

In a few days, they were aboard a four-motor amphibious plane. Finally, they were told their destination: Iwo Jima. But first, they had stops to make, island hopping to refuel at Johnson Island and Guam, among others. Finally, a Navy ship in sight, they landed on the water and transferred to a small rubber craft with their communications equipment.

The ship was huge and those on board barely noticed when the men climbed aboard with the waterproofed equipment strapped to their backs. A few officers seemed to know who they were and what they were there for.

They changed ships twice, going first from Guam to Saipan and then from Saipan to Tinian. And then there was one more transfer, to yet another rubber raft in the middle of nowhere.

My father recalled being grateful that the day was clear, the ocean calm. It was in stark contrast to what was to come.

I stared at my father as he leaned back, clearly finished with his story for the day. He looked exhausted.

"Wow," I said. "I had no idea, Dad."

"Well, that's because I didn't tell you," he said.

"I don't even know what to say."

"And now, it's time for a nap," he announced.

"I think I need one too," I said.

He laughed a little and then stood up wearily. But this time he didn't wait for me to leave. He walked past me and slowly up the stairs to his bedroom.

Back at home, although it was the middle of the day, I curled up on my bed next to my kitty, covering myself with a knitted blanket my aunt made me when I was in high school. Somehow his story had exhausted me. I could only imagine how he must have felt. My imagination ran away with me. I could see the whole story replaying in my mind. The last thought I had before falling asleep was, *He must have been so scared.*

CHAPTER NINE

Searching for Answers

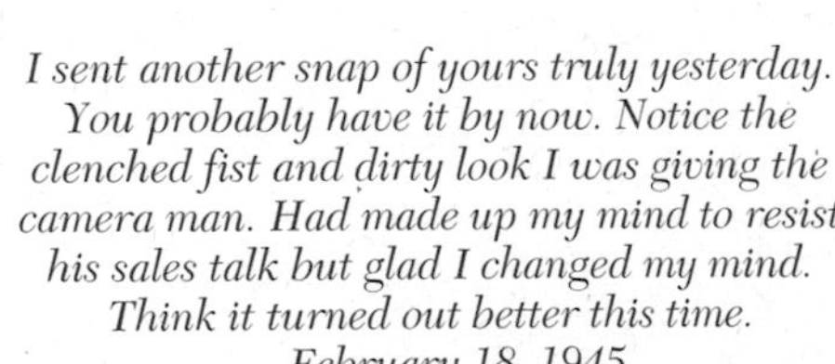

I sent another snap of yours truly yesterday. You probably have it by now. Notice the clenched fist and dirty look I was giving the camera man. Had made up my mind to resist his sales talk but glad I changed my mind. Think it turned out better this time.

—February 18, 1945

I awoke with a start, surprised I'd slept so well. Cocoa hadn't moved and as I stirred a little, she started to purr. I lay there for a while, petting her. Then my eyes rested on the WWII reference book I'd bought months earlier. It was oversized and sat on the shelf closest to the floor. I stretched as I got up. Cocoa did too. As my mind awoke, the conversation of a few hours before came back to me. He'd shared so much information that I hardly knew where to start. And even though he'd stopped mid-story, what he'd said finally gave me a place to start.

Until now, until my father told me about jungle warfare and the training before Iwo Jima, I hadn't known what I was looking for in the letters. The stories I grew up hearing didn't include Iwo Jima. They didn't include breaking a code called Katakana. And they didn't include any kind of intrigue or danger. But now? Now I knew there was something more. If I could find the letters he'd been ordered to write ahead of time, maybe then I could figure out what was going on.

I opened my dog-eared WWII reference book to the page that said Iwo Jima. The initial invasion was on February 19, 1945. To the best of his recollection, he was there a few days before that. So February 14 seemed like a good place to start in the letters.

"There has to be a clue here," I whispered.

I read with new resolve. He'd told me that because all outgoing mail was censored, he hadn't written home about what he was doing. So I was looking for other clues.

I opened the notebook to the letters written during that block of time. *Wouldn't it be amazing if I discovered something right here in his letters?* I thought. *Something that led me to the truth that was buried so deep within my father that even he couldn't find it?* Maybe a clue here would lead me to something I could use to help him find peace. Although he'd been told not to reveal anything about what he was doing in his letters, I knew my father. He was clever. If there was a way to secretly reveal something in his letters, he would have found a way to do it. So while I read each word, each sentence and paragraph, I also searched between the lines.

Feb 16, 1945

Dear Folks,

Just back from noon mail-call. No mail. I know now I have some coming tho as one of the mailmen said he saw some for me at my other address. Should get forwarded soon. I'm having quite a time with my mail.

Finished some washing a little while ago. Dad and Gerry can skip these details. Have a new system now. I just send my white blouse and trousers to laundry. They are a little slow so I wash all the other clothes myself. I have a five gallon can with top cut out and wire handle attached. I fill it with hot or cold water and put in some Rinso powdered soap and about a cup of Purex and mix well. Then put all my underwear, handkerchiefs, mattress cover, pillow case and towels in. Then begins the fun. I have one of the more modern methods for washing. Have a short broomstick with a red rubber suction cup on the end. By inserting this in the basket and vigorously working it up and down, the clothes seem to come out nice and white. I hang them on the line in back of the tent about 10 a.m. and by 5 p.m. they are good and dry and ready to bring in. Quite a system huh? When I get married I'm going to buy a wash board I believe. I think that would be much easier on the wife.

Studied more on my course—should finish first lesson tonite. I really enjoy it. Sure is going to make things easier and more understandable even on an agency job .

Well guess I'll close for now. Love, Murray

Feb 18, 1945

Dear Folks,

Lots of mail today so I'll have some to answer at least. No use you guys getting flustered 'cause I don't get my mail—about the time I start getting mail again, yours start arriving with sympathies etc. It really doesn't matter too much as it's all bound to catch up sooner or later anyway.

Nope, didn't hear of Japan's earthquake. All the news we get is what we hear on the radio and in papers. Just as well be in the middle of Tennessee as far as getting news is concerned. Every now and then the earth shakes like jelly but usually someone doing some blasting or anti-aircraft fire practice.

Glad you're getting some visitors. There are plenty of folks you take for granted until you get away from them.

Got a two page letter from Ray that was really newsy. He said it was the first letter he'd ever written that was over one page.

As for a birthday present—it sure won't be long now. Not a single thing I could use, except a good pen and pencil set. Just deposit a couple bucks or war stamps for me in your sock. Say, would you like me to subscribe to a Honolulu paper for you? Doesn't cost much and they tell a lot about our activities here that would be quite interesting to you. Of course the news and funnies would be quite old. Let me know. I can get it to you very easily. Might just try it for three months or something.

Went to church this morning. Have a real swell, down-to-earth lieutenant for a chaplain. He looks more like a run down section foreman than a Chaplain tho.

Sent my first traffic lesson in and starting on second today.

Better get a line off to Ray. Haven't received the foto album nor radio yet but it's probably in my old mail and will come in a bunch one of these days. Write—Love, Murray

Feb 19, 1945

Dear Folks,

'Twill be something new to get a V-mail from me. If you get it. Nothing new today. Got a valentine card today. That was all. Got to get ready for "Arsenic and Old Lace" in town pretty

quick. We all meet at the transportation office and get on a couple trucks and ride in and back. Should be a good show. I'll tell you if it is or not later.

Get kind of lonesome with Jonesy up at the hospital. I can't visit him very often and all by myself in the tent. Of course he isn't sick at all so he doesn't especially need comfort. They have him in a bed with a solid board under a thin mattress. Says he feels worse than he ever did as far as back is concerned.

I sent another snap of yours truly yesterday. You probably have it by now. Notice the clenched fist and dirty look I was giving the camera man. Had made up my mind to resist his sales talk but glad I changed my mind. Think it turned out better this time. My feet still go North and South as Ray says.

Be glad when the radio and foto album get here.

Write. Love, Murray

I read each letter again and again, through February 19. Then I worked backward to February 1. I studied his handwriting. I even looked at the first letters of his sentences, hoping to discover some kind of code, a secret hidden in the letters. Maybe it was something that even my grandparents had missed. I looked at the dates, the signatures. But there was nothing—absolutely nothing about code breaking, secret training, or the fact that he'd been sent off on a top-secret mission. There wasn't even a break in the letters.

I lay back on the bed, hours later. Only then did I feel the tension I'd held in my back and shoulders. They were stiff and aching.

"What are you doing?" I said aloud.

I so wanted the letters to read like an autobiography of my

father's wartime experiences. I wanted to discover the truth in his letters. I wanted to understand.

I kneaded my neck until my fingers hurt. And I suddenly wished I hadn't told my father that I was going to reread his letters from the time just prior to Iwo Jima.

After bursting through the story that day, my father quickly after became unsure. He had always been able to rely so confidently on his amazing memory, that to have a forgotten story come to him from what seemed like nowhere made him start to doubt whether the story was even true.

I'd told him, though, that I was sure I could find his whole story, or at least important parts of it, in his letters. I was so sure he would have talked about it in some way. It fit with what I knew about him. After all, it was likely that he had at least considered the notion that he might not return from this mission alive. He would have wanted his folks to know what he was doing if that were the case. I was just so sure that I knew him.

But now that I saw the answers weren't there, I wished I hadn't told him that there just *had* to be some kind of reference to the secret mission in his letters. Because I knew he'd ask. And he did.

I didn't go over to his house that week. I deluded myself into thinking that if enough time passed, he'd forget to ask me about what I'd read. But I couldn't avoid him forever. So the next Wednesday, on our regular day, I drove out to pick him up.

He'd just gotten a cell phone and learned how to text, so our new routine was that I sent a quick text saying, "omw," meaning "on my way." Then when I turned the corner on his street, I'd send another that said, "corner." He was just coming out the door when I pulled in the driveway. We exchanged our usual greetings and started driving to Mr. Ed's.

I'd only driven a few houses from his when he asked the question I'd been dreading all week.

"Did you reread those letters?" he asked.

"Yeah," I answered.

Silence followed.

"You find anything?" he asked.

"No," I said. "I didn't find anything."

I tried to explain.

"I even looked for things like a break in the letters you sent. I looked for a discrepancy or some kind of a secret reference to Iwo Jima."

"And you didn't find anything," he said.

Another silence. The thing about these car conversations was that we could talk without worrying about nonverbal communication. He couldn't search my eyes and I didn't have to see the disappointment in his.

"It was just so drilled into our heads," he said. "We knew everything was censored. But when that sergeant told us we'd be shot if anything leaked out, I just didn't...I didn't even have to think about it. I'm sure it didn't even occur to me to write about it to my folks. I don't think you'll ever find anything in those letters."

There was sadness in his voice now. He looked down.

"Maybe I was never there," he said. "You know the other night I was thinking, maybe I made all this up. Maybe I was holed up in a cabin in the Blue Mountains above Dayton during the war. Then when it was over, I came back down and lived my life just like before."

"That's ridiculous," I said.

"Maybe," he replied. "Maybe not."

He was giving up. Faced with the possibility that there wasn't concrete evidence that he'd been where he remembered being and experienced what he thought he'd experienced, it was easier for him to chalk it up to being an old man who made the whole thing up. I knew that wasn't true. And inside, I believed he knew that wasn't true too. Still, he'd put a period at the end of the sentence. But just because there's a period, doesn't mean the story's over.

Whether it came from his letters or someplace else, my father needed validation. Having me, his daughter, believe him, wasn't enough. He needed it in black and white. I so wanted to give him that. But I didn't know how I could after all these years.

CHAPTER TEN

Limbo

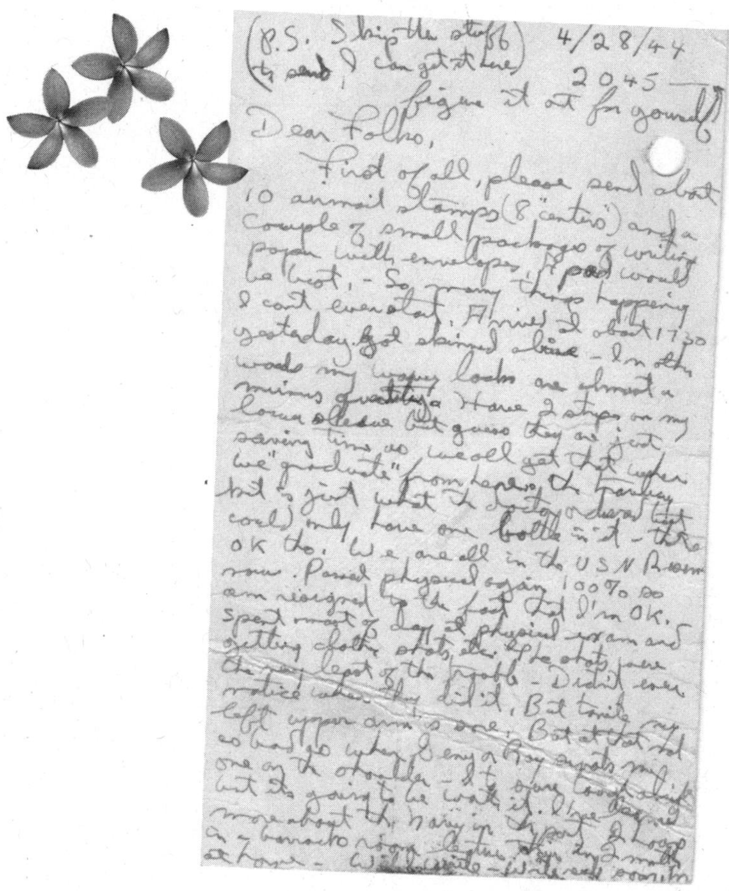

(P.S. Skip the stuff to send, I can get it here) 4/28/44
2045 — figure it out for yourself!

Dear Folks,

First of all, please send about 10 airmail stamps (8 "centos") and a couple of small packages of writing paper with envelopes, if pad would be best. — So many things happening I can't even start. Arrived at about 1730 yesterday. Got skinned alive — In other words my wavy locks are almost a minimus quantity. Have 2 stripes on my [illegible] but guess they are just saving time as we all get that when we "graduate" from here. The [illegible] but is just what the doctor ordered but could only have one bottle in it — that's OK tho. We are all in the USN Reserve now. Passed physical again 100% so am resigned to the fact that I'm OK. Spent most of day at physical exam and getting clothes, shots, etc. The shots were the very least of the trouble — Didn't even notice when they did it. But tonite my left upper arm is sore. But at that not so bad so when I [illegible] one on the shoulder — It [illegible] but it's going to be worth it. I['ll] [illegible] more about the navy in [illegible] [illegible] in a barracks room [illegible] at home — [illegible] — write [illegible]

I take my Shaeffer "triumph" pen,
which cost twenty-two bucks, in hand
and go to work. I'm getting so darned
swamped with mail nowadays.
—February 23, 1945

For a while, after not finding validation in his letters, my father and I didn't talk about the war. The disappointment ran deep for both of us, but especially for him. I could see it whenever we were together—the deep, deep sadness.

At home, the letters sat on the shelf untouched. I searched the Internet for information on code breaking and Iwo Jima. But searches on code breaking always pointed to the Native American code breakers. And information on Iwo Jima was common and well-documented history. I bought books on Iwo Jima and I spent hours at the library reading history books. I went to bookstores and sat with piles of WWII books, searching the table of contents and indexes for reference to Katakana. But my research wasn't getting anywhere.

When we were together, my father and I didn't know what to say. Anything that I rehearsed just sounded like I was making excuses for him. What I wanted to say was, "I believe you, Dad. And I don't need to read it in your letters or anywhere else." But even that sounded inadequate. So I said nothing. And neither did he. We talked about anything *but* the war, avoiding it all.

I wanted to know the rest of the story, though. He'd simply stopped talking at a crucial part. I pictured him as a young sailor, in the middle of the ocean on a calm day. I wanted to know what happened next. But it seemed that every time I tried to help, things only got worse. So we simply ate our breakfast each week while we talked about other things. It was always on my mind. But I learned that I could pretend too.

I found myself spending more and more time in my favorite place in our home, a room that wasn't a room at all. In fact, it wasn't even *in* the house. Our large, covered front porch, which ran the entire length of the front of our house, was the heart of our home. It was the place where our children grew up and where we did too. Memories took up residence there, like tiny droplets of dew on the spring tulips below. I had wonderful memories of my grandmother's porch, one almost identical to mine. My sisters and I spent many childhood hours playing with our cousins there.

Built in 1907, the craftsman style house was my dream home. I fell in love with it from the outside in. It didn't hurt that the first time we saw it, it was Christmastime and adorned with colorful lights all the way up to the top of the second-story roof.

It was a few days before Christmas 1990, and we were driving around town looking at the Christmas lights, a family tradition. We drove past a house with a large front porch like my grandmother's. As our two young children craned their necks, oohing and awing at the lights from the backseat, I saw the sign I'd been looking for: a *for sale* sign. And I just knew, that this house would be not only our first home, but the only home we'd ever need.

I sat on the porch swing one afternoon, gliding back and forth. It was a perfect place to people watch. And the best thing was that those who strode by rarely knew I was there. Tucked back a bit from the street, it simply didn't occur to them that someone might be watching. Not even the rhythmic creak of the porch swing caught their attention.

My mind wandered, my thoughts easily going to my father. I was lulled once again into a mode of what I should have said, what I should have done, how I could have handled the situation differently, so that I wouldn't have hurt him.

I was so deep in my thoughts that when I spotted my father, at first I thought it was just part of my daydream. But then I sat up as I saw it was really him.

He stood on his Segway, rounding the corner toward our house. He let go with one hand and waved. Then he cut across the street and rode up the sidewalk, stopping just short of the steps. Stepping off the platform of the stand-up scooter, he leaned it against the railing and climbed the stairs. He sat down on the wicker chair across from me with a loud sigh.

"You want a glass of water or something?" I asked.

"Oh, how about a *something*?" he joked.

"OK. *Something*, coming right up," I said.

I went to the kitchen and filled a glass with ice and water, taking a moment for a deep breath. I knew I had to somehow break the moratorium on all things WWII, even if it was just a baby step. So I stood there, glass of water in hand, and I prayed, "God help me." It was a silly and cliché prayer, but I meant it.

I pushed the screen door open with my elbow and handed

Dad his water as the door clunked shut. Sitting back down, I stuffed a pillow behind my back.

Keep it simple, I thought.

After some small talk about the weather, the Seattle Mariners game last night, and the newest information he'd learned in the Segway chatroom, he was all talked out. So, after a brief silence, I gathered all the courage I could muster.

"Hey, Dad," I said. "You sure did talk about cars a lot in your letters."

He smiled, then took a long, slow drink of water. He set the glass on the small wrought-iron table beside him.

"I was probably just running out of things to say," he said. "After arriving on Oahu and then a few weeks of describing it, I suppose there wasn't much else to talk about. And cars were really a big deal back then."

He talked then for a half hour about his cars. But it wasn't about the subject really; it was about talking again. It was a teeny, tiny baby step, but our communication lines were open once again.

Later, I watched him ride his Segway past our neighbor's house on the corner, a two-story craftsman like ours. The young children playing in the front yard stopped momentarily to watch him ride smoothly down the sidewalk and around the corner. He waved without looking back. After setting our glasses in the sink, I took the letters down from the shelf for the first time in days.

Feb 23, 1945

Dear Folks,

I take my Shaeffer "triumph" pen, which cost twenty-two bucks, in hand and go to work. I'm getting so darned swamped with mail nowadays. I'm just about snowed under. Got one from you and it only took four days to get here. Nothing new to write about.

Saw Fibber and Molly in "Heavenly Days" last night and visited Jonesy a little.

Still hot as blazes although we have had a little rain now and then. Doesn't stay cool tho. About all I can say for it, is that it's real cool at night so I can sleep good.

I told Ray to collect my tax refund and spend it foolishly on the Cord. Eighty bucks too.

From the sound of things about the Fiat, I'd just about bet you even money I end up fixing it myself. Sure is slow going when you can't get any cooperation from mechanics. After working on such a mess as a Ford V8 that little Fiat should be easy as duck soup. That motor is about as simple as they come. I know when it was running it started so quick that you hardly heard the starter at all.

Suppose you've heard all about Iwo Jima by now. Quite an operation huh? Doubt if any of my gang got there in time for any of it. Of course that's kind of out of our line anyway.

Write. Love, Murray

And there it was. Just like that.

When I took a break from reading the letters, I'd somehow

expected that the letters too, or at least the story contained in them, would be taking a break. It was as if I'd expected my father, fifty years earlier, to be in his Quonset hut, lying on his bunk, waiting for me to continue the journey of reading his letters. So when I picked them up again, it was without any expectation at all.

But suddenly, there it was; the reference I was searching so hard for was right there in the letter dated February 23, 1945.

Granted, it wasn't much. But I knew Dad would be pleased that I found something. If this letter had something, it was conceivable that others did too. Perhaps in others he would elaborate.

It was late, but I picked up the phone and dialed his number.

"Hi, Dad," I said. "I just thought I'd tell you that I found a reference to Iwo Jima in your letters."

"Really?" he asked.

I could tell he was surprised. His voice had a tiny lilt to it—something that only after months of conversation had I come to recognize and describe as something between joy and relief.

"Yeah," I continued. "You said that you supposed your folks heard about Iwo Jima by now and that you doubted if any of the gang got there in time for it."

"Well!" he said and then there was a long pause. "Maybe I wasn't hiding in the hills after all."

"Good night, Dad," I said.

"Good night," he said. But before I'd pulled the receiver from my ear, he added, "Thanks."

My father felt validated. I don't know how I knew that, but I did. It was something he needed. It didn't matter that his family believed him. He needed to see it written down.

I wondered if this was all there was to this odyssey. Maybe

it was about getting his secrets about code breaking out in the open where they could be validated. Could it be as simple as that? I didn't know.

For now, though, I was just thankful for an answer—no matter how small. When I lay my head on the pillow that night, I was satisfied that I'd finally brought some little bit of peace to my father. What I didn't know was that doubt would soon come crashing down on me.

CHAPTER ELEVEN

Nightmares Return

DRIVER'S PERMIT
NavDist 14-119

NAME

Nº 109693

FISHER. M. W.

Rank-Rate: RM3c

Badge-Serial No.

ISSUING COMMAND

AD COM PHIBS PAC.

Date Issued: 11/13/45

Date Expires: EMERG

This is to certify that the holder of this permit has been (examined and) found qualified to operate Navy-owned vehicles as hereon indicated.

(FILL IN ALL SPACES WITH WORD "YES or NO")

(YES) Vehicles Not Exceeding ¾-Ton Load Capacity

(NO) Truck Not To Exceed......... Tons Load Capacity

(NO) Passenger Bus

(NO) Tractor-Trailer Passenger Unit

(NO) Truck Tractor-Trailer Not To Exceed.............Tons Load Capacity

Signature of Issuing Officer

V. W. LANGWORTHY,
Flag Secretary.

Signature of Examiner

(See Reverse Side)

My address is Ad.Com.Phib.Pac., which is merely an abbreviation for Administrative Command Amphibious Pacific—which is just what we wanted to stay out of.—January 22, 1945

The mention of Iwo Jima was just that, a mention. It wasn't anything personal, like, "I was there." Still, I had renewed energy and motivation to keep searching.

The following Wednesday I was a little early picking Dad up for our regular breakfast. As Dad went to shave and get his coat for breakfast, Mom motioned for me to go outside with her. We stood on the brick steps.

"The nightmares have started again," she said.

She looked at me as if I was an expert in this field, as if she'd asked a question that only I could answer.

"Really?" I asked.

My mind went back to the first nightmares. Shortly after 9/11, my father had become depressed. He didn't realize it at the time and it's only on reflection that my mother and I put it together, but somehow his WWII experiences got linked with the tragedy of 9/11. Soon, he immersed himself in everything having to do with WWII. Then the nightmares began. They weren't specific at all. But to him, they were real and troubling.

As he tossed and turned, my mother would feel the bed move. His screams came out as pathetic whimpers. If she tried to wake him, it seemed to make it worse. Then he'd wake with a start and sit on the side of the bed, sweating profusely. But he never remembered what the night terrors were about, only a general sense that they were about the war.

Then for no obvious reason at all, they stopped. It was sometime after that he gave me the letters.

My mother twisted her wedding ring.

"I wonder why they've started again," I said.

I wanted to help. I wanted to offer something to her, like she'd done for me so many times over the years. Still, my father's reaction baffled me. Was it just chance that the nightmares started again? Was it the mere mention of Iwo Jima? What else could there be? He still hadn't told me anything about what he did there. My mother stared at me. I wanted to help; I just didn't know how.

"He was restless and calling out in his sleep last night," she said. "I couldn't understand what he was saying, but he just tossed and turned all night long. In the morning, when I picked his pajamas up off the floor to throw them in the dirty clothes, the top was just drenched with sweat. I mean, you could practically wring it out it was so wet."

Just then, my father appeared at the screen door. He frowned at my mother.

"Oh, you stop talking to her, Bettye," he said. "Wednesdays are for me. You're not allowed to speak on Wednesdays, don't you know that?"

At breakfast, I watched for signs. I expected him to ask about the reference to Iwo Jima that I'd found in his letter. After we ordered our food, there was a lull in our conversation. But he didn't bring it up, so I decided not to bring it up either.

When I dropped him back at his house, the whole breakfast

had come and gone without him saying a single word about it. And that made me wonder: What had changed? Why wasn't he anxious to talk about it now?

That evening, while watching the news, an image came on the screen. It was a report on the war in Iraq—dusty roads, abandoned buildings, and U.S. soldiers who wore so much gear that even their mothers wouldn't recognize them. They were on a rooftop lying in wait. They were on their bellies or squatting by glassless windows. Suddenly, gunfire erupted from the abandoned buildings.

I jumped, startled from my armchair complacency. I quickly took the remote control from the coffee table, my thumb over the channel button. I froze. I couldn't change the channel.

The men on the screen couldn't change it either. I imagined how the pound of bullets escaping guns, the sound that I could simply turn up or down, must feel in their chest. I held my heart and tears welled in my eyes.

And so it goes, I thought sadly. Generation to generation. War to war. My daddy's pain, held in for so many years, was the same as any soldier returning from war today. On the screen, the gunfire had stopped. The team, who could easily have just died, was jubilant. *For now,* I thought. *For now you are joyful. But what will you be when you are back on U.S. soil and that joy is a lifetime away? What will your life be like then?*

I felt so sad that I simply went to bed. I wanted to not think about what I'd seen. But I couldn't stop thinking. My father had come home from the war like everyone else of that era. He'd returned to the soil of his home just as the soldiers today would do. But somehow a part of his soul remained there. Something had happened there, and even though his mind may have pushed it aside, buried it, his soul had not.

I finally fell into a deep sleep. It was a dreamless sleep, but also one without memories that turned to nightmares as I slept. I was one of the lucky ones.

CHAPTER TWELVE

When I Get Home

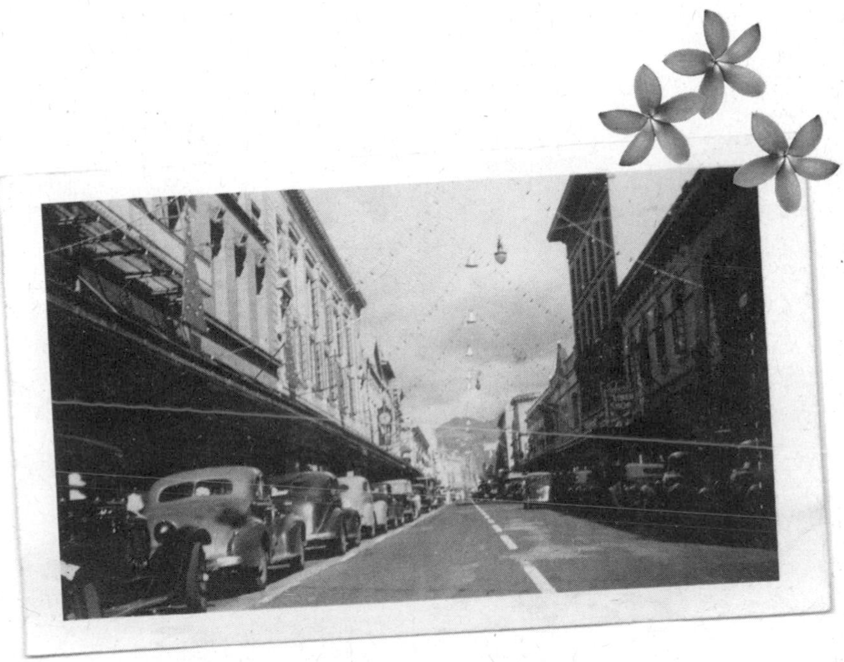

We went through the best part of town…Very nice houses and a Sears store is located way out on the edge of town. It's a super-modern, one-story building as are most of the large stores in town.—February 9, 1945

Once again, my father wasn't talking to me about the war. It was a strange turn. In such a short time, we'd gone from the joy of finding a bit of information that he seemed happy about, to the nightmares starting again. But I didn't let much time pass. After just a few weeks, I made a decision: whether my father was willing or able to talk with me, I'd trudge ahead with reading the letters. This time, I wasn't going to stop reading while he wasn't talking.

I would simply take notes and ask him questions later, when he *was* up to talking. And if he never talked about it again, that would have to be OK too. I may have told myself this. But I don't think I ever really believed it. What I really believed was that something was haunting my father. I couldn't imagine what it might be. I also believed that this thing we'd started, this journey, there had to be a reason for it. There had to be a purpose.

Feb 26, 1945

Dear Folks,

Don't believe I'll ever get caught up on all my letter writing. Have been writing an average of about three a day since I've been here—including your daily one (almost). My friend from over headquarters way brought me six older ones last night from that letter famine of a couple of weeks ago. Five from you.

Whatever you do, don't sell the Fiat. I want it to play with if you get tired of it.

At last heard all about the seat on the flivver anyway. Sure sounds like you did a good job Gerry. Keep it up and you'll be just as good as your big brother some day. Now that's really a high mark to shoot for. Just hope you can get in the car—you say you haven't tried it yet. Remember the guy that built the boat in the basement!

And Gerry, I wouldn't say Larry Flanagan has "all the luck." They just love to get guys about his age. Give 'em a commission and then drop 'em behind enemy lines somewhere. We have a lot of Ensigns in the Navy that are younger than I am. They look to be 19 or 20, most of them. They just practically shoot themselves at the Japs.

As long as you know what island I'm on now and what I'm doing (mostly) I guess it's O.K. Of course this whole place is alive with everything in the way of fighting goods and men. That's the kind of stuff that is censored so will have to wait until I get back. Of course I can tell you what I do presently as long as it doesn't go into military aspects (and there sure are plenty here).

Such hours you night owls keep—1:30 am. What's this older generation coming to! You'll have to kind of keep mom and dad in check Gerry. I like to get those Northern Pacific bulletins dad. I think when I get back I'll just bid on something on every bulletin and see the whole division. Live in a trailer house.

Also think I'm going to write Mr. B.E. Nason at St. Paul and ask him about bidding on job while in service. I don't think it can be done but looks like it isn't quite fair if we can't. Also going to ask him if they can or will allow me to take a leave of absence when I get out, to go to school or if I could work for a while first and then go. I would like to take advantage of the G.I. Bill of Rights. I think that could probably be arranged.

Oh well, that's probably a day or so off yet. Someone says we're going to be in Tokyo a year from now. That's still too long to suit me.

Write. Love, Murray

So my father planned to tell his family all about it when he got back. Maybe he did. Now was as good a time as any to find out. Although he still didn't seem to want to talk, there were other people who just might. Both of my grandparents passed away long ago but he had three siblings. Of Dad's two brothers and one sister, his brother Raymond was the most likely to have the information I was looking for.

Raymond was a retired Certified Public Accountant who spent every spare moment he had researching genealogy. He'd traced our own family line back a few hundred years and then went to work on other people's. It was his passion. He lived 150 miles away in Spokane, Washington, but he was always prompt in his responses to emails. So, I sent him one. In it, I asked what he remembered about what my father did during the war and about his homecoming. I hit send and stared at the "your message has been sent" screen.

Then I thought about my Aunt Iris. She lived just a mile or so down the road and I hadn't seen her in a while. I was due for a visit anyway, so I grabbed my car keys and purse from the bird-shaped hook behind the door, and hopped in my car. Before starting the car, I checked my purse to be sure my small notebook was still there.

Iris opened the door smiling. She was quick to grab me a Pepsi as we passed through the kitchen. Even now, nearing her eighties, she was the kind of person who always made a point of keeping your favorites stocked up, just in case you dropped by.

In the living room, she sat next to a wicker basket that was overflowing with pastel-colored yarns. She'd knitted for as long as I could remember and that basket always held her most recent project.

"Who's the blanket for?" I asked.

"Oh, a girl from church who's having a baby," she said.

That was Iris, always doing something for others. She'd even volunteered to make tiny hats for the newborn babies at the hospital.

"It's pretty," I said.

She pulled the half-finished blanket to her lap, and gently spread the yarn apart.

"Oh, it isn't very good at all. See, this part here is smaller than this part," she replied.

I'd learned not to argue with her. The things she made were

beautiful, perfect. But she was humble to a fault, not wanting any adulation for it.

"Well, that little baby will love it," I said. "You know, I've been transcribing Dad's letters from WWII," I explained.

"I heard."

Her knitting needles clicked every now and then as she kept her hands busy while we talked.

"Oh, you did?" I asked.

"Murray told me you were doing that," she said.

"Well, I have a question for you then."

"OK. I doubt I can answer it though," she replied.

When she looked down, watching her hands as she continued to knit, I took out my notebook and a pen.

"Did you know what Dad did during the war?" I asked.

"You mean the code-breaking thing?"

I nodded.

"Oh, I suppose I did. Well, I guess I knew he did something with code, but I'm not sure. But that's about *all* I knew. We didn't really talk about it," she said.

I waited but there was no elaboration.

"In one of the letters to his folks, he said that he'd tell them what he did during the war after he got home."

Iris thought for a moment, her knitting needles moving rhythmically.

"Well, everything in letters back then was censored, you know. He was probably afraid of getting into trouble if he said something he wasn't supposed to," she said.

Perfect, I thought. It was just the transition I needed.

"So, what about when he got back?" I asked. "What did he say about what he'd done during the war? Do you remember?"

"I don't remember him saying anything at all," she replied. "It was just a different time. We were all just glad the war was over and we could get back to our lives."

"Yeah, I suppose that was probably true for a lot of people," I said.

"You know," she added, "the men who returned from the war, they just didn't want anything except to get their jobs back and get back to work. They didn't want anything special."

What I'd learned about my father fit perfectly with what she was saying. But it hadn't occurred to me quite that way before. To him it really was just ancient history; they *were* just old letters and an old man's story. He'd probably been so happy to return from the war alive that he simply went back to his prewar life. The things that had seemed so important during the war must have felt as far away as the miles between war and home. In that context, it made sense that he'd promised something in his letters that he never fulfilled when he got home. It simply hadn't mattered to him anymore.

As we finished our conversation, I put my notebook and pen back in my purse, as inconspicuously as possible, without writing a word.

Back home, I checked my email and Raymond had not only responded, but he'd also called my other uncle, Gerald, in Hawaii to confer. But the information he shared was identical to what Iris had just said. Even after a few more prodding questions over a few more days, the end result was the same. My father had come home from the war and simply gone back to work. Neither of them even remembered any special dinner or celebration of any kind. It was as if he simply stepped back into his life after the war.

What must have felt right at the time, and was a reflection of the times, left many questions for those of us who didn't live through it—especially those who were born years after it. In many cases those questions would remain unanswered forever. In the process of gathering information and sharing with others about the journey, I'd heard many a sad story. People shared their guilt and disappointment over not getting their father, or mother in some cases, to talk about their war experiences. Sometimes their stories would come on their deathbed. Sometimes they'd come after death, when letters or memorabilia were found, leaving the child with the unbearable burden of always wondering if there was something they should have said or done to encourage their loved ones to tell stories of their past. But their parents' heroism was discovered too late.

My father's siblings knew Dad had done work in naval intelligence and with some kind of a code, but that was all.

I'd hit the familiar brick wall once again. But I resolved to keep on trying to climb it.

CHAPTER THIRTEEN

Pieces

Well, we lost some more of the gang yesterday...Took us off alphabetically to the Mc's and so that cut us in two again.—January 9, 1945

My life was full of the joys of parenting: sleepovers, football games, school dances, driver's ed, family camping trips, and on and on. And in between, at least on our appointed day of Wednesday, I met with my father. Each Wednesday was a reminder that even with all the progress we'd made, we still had a long way to go. And no matter how each day went, we always found ourselves ready to try again the next week.

Dad continued to feed me little bits of information. But there was nothing sequential about his memories. I likened it to taking the pages of a book and cutting them into sentences or paragraphs and then randomly giving you a passage here and there, with no assurance that you would ever get the whole book. And my job was to organize the pieces so that I could plug them in later, when—if—I ever knew the whole story.

I was learning when to push and when to back off. It was a delicate balance, and one that often, because of my own impatience, got off kilter.

Sometimes he didn't want to talk and I simply didn't have a new question to ask. But as long as we kept meeting once a week, we were both happy.

Still, I often imagined his story up until the abrupt halt in information he'd shared with me. In my mind's eye, it was like watching a television show. I saw a young man from a small farming community being trained to break a top-secret code. He then sat and waited as the war seemed to pass him by. After a few more scenes and a few commercial breaks, the action picked up again. Things were moving much more quickly now. I saw him climbing from a rubber raft up a steep ladder to board a Navy ship in the middle of the ocean. But then the story stopped. The power went off.

My thoughts were divided: I knew that talking about what is troubling you is good. So I wanted that for my father. But I didn't know where his breaking point was. And there wasn't any manual for that.

All the while, life around me just kept moving forward. The kids still needed braces in the fall. Football practice was about to start. And homework had to be done every night.

At our weekly breakfasts though, for an hour or two I could focus on just one thing: my dad. And regardless of the subject, regardless of whether we were talking about his *story* or not, it was, for me, a break from being torn in different directions. I'd learned to be content with silence. I busied myself with moving forward reading his letters and transcribing them. When the time was right, either he would start talking again or I would ask questions again. I was beginning to believe in my intuitive sense for timing.

After breakfast one morning, my dad and I ran a few errands. We went through the drive-through to refill my prescription and then to the home improvement store. My father was like a kid in a candy store at Home Depot. He'd wander up and down the aisles looking for some new gadget or a specific piece of something for his latest project at home. We went our separate ways at the door, me to the gardening section and him to everything else.

He was quiet on the way home—worn out, I supposed. As I turned the corner to his street, he asked if I'd mind coming in. He had something for me to read.

"It's in here," he said, leading me to the sunroom.

I felt a sense of déjà vu. It had been a long time since he'd placed the notebooks full of letters on my lap, and in that very same room.

I moved a needlepoint pillow as I sat on the corner sofa. He handed me a book. It was Tom Brokaw's *The Greatest Generation Speaks*. Then he reached down, opening it to a page marked by a yellow sticky note.

"The first paragraph," he said.

He walked across the room and sat on an antique chair.

I looked down at the book. The text was set apart, a quote.

"Don't read it out loud," he said. "I can't…"

He didn't finish his sentence. I began reading.

Most of those who survived know it was simply fate that saved them. Their buddies a few feet to the left and to the right were fatally wounded. The survivors carry that with them to this day; they are still asking, "Why did I survive?" Every day and every opportunity is a dividend their fallen comrades never realized. One man wrote to me about his father, a World War II combat veteran who had lost many young friends in battle. Recalling those who didn't live beyond their twenties, the dying man said to his son, "Don't sing any sad songs for me, boy. I've had my life. I've seen my grandchildren. Don't sing any sad songs for me."

I stared at the page, absorbing the words. When I looked up, my father's eyes were on me, as if he'd been watching me as I read.

"This is how you feel?" I asked.

He nodded, ever so slightly.

That short paragraph gave words to my father's silent ache. But it also was a new beginning for us. It was clear that although my father had not been talking with me about the war, his thoughts had remained on it, just as mine had. Neither of us had truly taken a break from it. In fact, I presumed that it was now impossible to take a break from it. It was like a carnival ride that had already begun and it was too late to change your mind. There was only one thing to be done now, and that was to finish what we'd started.

"Do you mind if I take this home with me?" I asked. "I just want to make a copy of it."

"Sure," he said. "You can keep it. I'm done with it."

CHAPTER FOURTEEN

Pearl

SPECIAL PASS

U. S. Navy Yard, Pearl Harbor, Hawaii, U. S. A.

Expiring 31 March, 1946

No. 242 Date 4 January 1946

PASS FISHER, M.W. RM3c

In and out of MAIN GATE & Sub Base Gates

Out of hours in dungarees

W. G. Schmidt

Flag Detachment
Amphibious Forces,
U. S. Pacific Fleet.

You can't see a thing that would tell that the Japs bombed probably right on the spot I'm writing.—February 27, 1945

The letters dated after the invasion of Iwo Jima didn't have any clue about what had happened there. Neither did they offer any more information about my father's involvement. So, as I read through them, I was disappointed. And since my father wasn't really giving me any new details, I simply transcribed them. I had no new questions to ask. But that changed when I read the letter dated February 27, 1945.

Feb 27, 1945

Dear Folks,

Hooray—Received both radio and foto album yesterday. Both in excellent condition. Been just sitting looking through the album and listening to the radio. Didn't get any mail (letters), for the first time in about two weeks. With the album and radio I won't holler too much tho.

I really don't know what I'm going to find to write about if I keep this letter a day business up—may just cut it down to a page or two instead of three. Don't know what I'd do with my time if I didn't write letters.

Been up to see Jonesy. He's no worse or any better. I take him magazines and cigarettes and anything else he pays for. Still has no idea whether he will get out or stay in for a while. Doc says he doesn't know what to do with him. Jonesy says he could suggest something.

Saw "Gypsy Wildcat," with Maria Montez and Jon Hall last night. Had seen it in Spokane a long time ago but still, it was good. I see a different show every night.

One thing you might be interested in—all the stores carry all the advertised brands of goods that you see in the states. A lot are produced here in Honolulu with same trade name. Also have practically all the chain stores such as Safeway, Newberrys, Kresses and Sears.

Tomorrow is my liberty day. Didn't go on any extras this week at all. Kind of tired of going so often when it's such hard work to get to town and back. I'm allergic to work by now (Quiet Gerry).

By the way—You could kind of guess what my military location is—remember what happened a little over three years ago? Right. You'd sure never know it tho. You can't see a thing that would tell that the Japs bombed probably right on the spot I'm writing.

Just about thru a lesson on railroad freight classification. So far it's just a résumé of all the railroad procedure. Course seems to be a lot of study of tariff and reasons for various rules and orders. Just what I always wanted to study. Have a long way to go yet tho. It's really thorough.

Say mom, I may take over your job for that 90 days when I come back. Wouldn't want to go to Helix and mess things up at first. Wouldn't matter at Dayton—they'd just blame it on the labor shortage and women.

By the way—I suppose you noticed the tube almost striking thru on the Fiats spare tire. Want to sell it yet Gerry? If so, don't you dare without first consulting me. I'm going to have one when I come back if I have to go buy one from Mussolini in Italy.

Write & rush those fotos of the Fiat. Love, Murray

My father's reference to Pearl Harbor made me think of a new direction to go with my questions. Since he hadn't actually been there on December 7, 1941, when Pearl Harbor was bombed, it was probably something he'd talk about. I waited until the next Wednesday to bring it up.

Mr. Ed's had become our touchstone. The former burger restaurant still had some of its original A&W appeal—large vinyl booths with telephones for ordering that were no longer connected. When the chain restaurant folded, Elvis moved in—quite literally. An eight-foot sculpture of Elvis, complete with guitar and swayed hip, was the first thing you saw when you entered.

After sitting down, you slowly began to notice that there was most definitely an Elvis theme throughout. Memorabilia was everywhere; every little nook and cranny had an Elvis something. The only variation was when, on the first day of a holiday month, seasonal decorations joined Elvis, from eggs and bunnies for Easter to Santa and his reindeer for Christmas, and everything in between.

But whether you were a fan of Elvis or not, it was the people who worked at Mr. Ed's who brought you back. Every employee, from the waitresses and busboys to the cooks, just had a way of making you feel like you just stepped into your grandmother's kitchen after a hard day's work. Still, Biby (pronounced bye-bee) was our favorite waitress. Every week the twenty-something girl greeted us like long-lost friends. Dad took a liking to her and he didn't like it when, for some reason, she either wasn't there or wasn't working our table. Still, she always made a point of giving him a hard time about one thing or another. She was the kind of waitress who would plop down beside you when she had a moment, just to see how life was going for you.

We always ordered the same thing: eggs Benedict. In fact, that's how we got our own bit of fame there, something Biby revealed to us. One day we had come in and Biby wasn't there. Dad complained half-jokingly to the waitress who took our order. The next day the waitress mentioned to her that "the Benedicts" had been there. Biby said she had to think for a bit to figure out who in the world the Benedicts were, and then she laughed.

After she told us this, every now and then, we'd hear someone joke about it. "Hey, Biby," they'd say, "the Benedicts are here."

The parking lot at Mr. Ed's was nearly full that morning, but I parked as close to the door as I could. Dad held the heavy door for me. There were two tables available, one in the center, by the fireplace, and one by the window.

"Which would you like?" Biby asked with a broad gesture.

"How about an ocean view?" Dad asked.

"You're so funny!" she said.

She looked out the window at the familiar view of the street, with the Blue Mountains in the background.

"So, which ocean are we lookin' at?" she teased.

"Oh, how about the Pacific? This is Hawaii, isn't it?" he asked.

"Hawaii? Sure it is. You look like you're ready for Hawaii, with that shirt and all," she said.

Dad loved Hawaii. He wore a button up Hawaiian shirt every spring and summer day, switching to plaid print flannel for the fall and winter. His brother Gerry had lived in Hawaii with his wife for many years. But for Dad it was more than just visiting his brother. He really loved the island and its people, a fact that seemed even more intriguing to me now.

We first went there in 1979, when I was a teenager. My sister Kathy and I were teenagers and my sister Susan was in her twenties. At the time, I don't think it even registered with me that we were standing on the very soil my father had been on during the war. I'm embarrassed by how out of touch I was. I was almost sixteen at the time, old enough to at least ask a few intelligent questions. But like most teenagers, I imagine, my memories are not of the cultural or historic places my parents took us to. My most vivid memories are of my sisters and me walking to the beach and spending hours there, in our bathing suits, in the warm ocean.

But there was another side to our trip: the extravagant and much more grown-up side. My Uncle Gerry, publisher of *The Beach Press*, was someone who it seemed *everyone* wanted to impress. We had valet parking, something I didn't know existed. In restaurants, we were seated at the table with the best view. At luaus and other activities, we never waited in a line. There were even VIP seats for us at the popular island attraction, The Polynesian Cultural Center. And I was only slightly embarrassed when some random family accidentally sat in them and was politely asked to move for us. Our small town in the Pacific Northwest afforded no such luxuries. After the family trip to Hawaii, my parents didn't go again until they retired.

Biby returned with a carafe of water.

"The usual?" she asked. "Two half Bennies and extra sauce for you?"

"Yep," my father said.

I poured water into the red plastic glasses.

"So, Dad, you were at Pearl Harbor a few years after its bombing, right? What was it like then?" I asked.

"Well, it wasn't like you'd imagine at all," he said. "By the time I got there, it was three years after the bombing. People didn't talk about it really. It was just a regular base to us."

"When we went on the Pearl Harbor tour when I was a teenager, I remember, we could still see oil leaking from the *Arizona*," I said.

"Yeah, well, we could see it during the war. They call it the black tears of the *Arizona*, or something like that now. You know, most of the guys who died down there were never taken out to be buried. They're still down there. Every time some group cries about environmental concerns or whatever, one veteran's group or another cries out louder. I'm sure the *Arizona* will never be brought up or moved."

He thought for a moment before continuing. "Well, not until we're all gone anyway. Then they'll just do whatever they want."

He paused, taking a drink of water. He'd said it so matter-of-factly. But his eyes betrayed him. The thought made him sad. He moved on before I could say anything—and before he could feel anything too deeply.

"One of my jobs while I was there was to get the mail," he said.

"Security was pretty strict, but I had a jeep pass, so I had a jeep at my disposal all the time, parked right outside our barracks. It was *supposed* to only be used for official business. Anyway, another guy and I would hop in our jeep and then drive across Pearl Harbor to a landing that handled the mail. We'd pick it up in these canvas sacks and then drop it at the post office for the amphibs. But the best part of the whole deal was that the only way to get to Ford Island was by boat. So, instead of a regular jeep, we had an amphibious jeep assigned to us."

"An amphibious jeep?" I asked. "You mean it was part boat and part jeep?"

"Well, sort of," he said.

He pulled a pen from his pocket and started to draw on the paper placemat.

"It was like a regular jeep in the guts of it," he explained, "but the body was more like a boat that slopes on both ends. There was no top but it did have a windshield, and it had a propeller in the back. All I had to do was drive down a ramp into the water, pull a lever to engage the propeller, and away we went."

He drew tiny details on what appeared to be the dashboard.

"All of the controls were pretty much like a car except it wouldn't go fast at all," he said. "It steered by just turning the wheels. The action of the wheels against the water made it turn, but slowly and with difficulty at times."

"So you weren't going to win any races?" I joked.

"No, but we had a great time with it. We used it all over the base," he said. "In fact, the *Arizona* still showed quite a bit above water at the time. They had ropes all around it to try to keep people away. When we were bored, we'd go over there and duck under the ropes and lean right up against the masts and turrets. We'd hang on to something and peer down into the water to see if we could see anything. I guess that sounds morbid now. But it's just what we did. There were other ships too that we looked over but none as famous as that one. They were still working on salvaging them. I always wished I had snuck a camera in with me and taken pictures but they were very strict about cameras. I always thought it would be fun to own one of those amphibious jeeps right now and run it around town and in parades and so forth. Maybe I will start looking for one!"

"I think you'd better check with Mom on that one," I said.

"Why would I want to do that? She'll just ruin all my fun," he said.

"Da-ad…" I mock scolded.

He laughed. We both did.

I'd been right. Talking about the part of the war he wasn't involved in was easier. These memories came easy. I was able to enjoy what he was telling me—not worrying about what I may be unknowingly unearthing. In fact, these stories were reminiscent of those I'd heard growing up. It had been a long, long time since I'd heard one of those stories. And now I could see that when he told them, his countenance was different, lighter. He was enjoying remembering. And that made me smile.

Biby returned with our steaming plates.

"You drew all over your placemat," she teased. "You want a new one?"

"Well, what do you mean? You don't like my art?" he asked.

"Oh, sure I do, sweetie," Biby said. "It's beautiful. I just thought maybe you'd want to save it for later. You know, put it up on your fridge or something."

My father laughed. And for the first time in a while, I felt warm inside.

CHAPTER FIFTEEN

Iwo Jima

A mob of new guys came in last night and chow line is about a mile long.—March 6, 1945

As the weeks went by, I often gave my father updates on my progress with the letters by telling him the date on the most recent letter and a few details about its contents. But a few months had passed since we'd talked about them in depth or I had asked him any questions.

My mother and I now checked in with each other regularly. She would let me know if Dad was having nightmares, or if she'd noticed his mood change. Likewise, I would share if we'd been talking about something that seemed to upset him. Sometimes there seemed to be a direct correlation. Other times, I couldn't see a link at all.

So when I would update him about the letters, I was careful not to include anything that might trigger nightmares for him. The problem with our system was that I didn't always know what the trigger was. Something that seemed benign could be something that wasn't at all benign. I was very careful with what I talked to him about.

But one Wednesday, as soon as we'd ordered our usual breakfast, he caught me off guard by asking *me* a question.

"So, how are the letters coming?" he asked.

For some reason, I didn't even think to filter things like I usually did. Maybe it was because it was he who asked the question, instead of me offering. Maybe I was just tired—maybe we both were. Whatever the case, the words *Iwo Jima* came tumbling out of my mouth.

"The letters I'm transcribing right now were probably written at about the time you went to Iwo Jima," I said.

As I had researched Iwo Jima, I had learned what a huge part of WWII it was. It made me wonder if Dad's military records might hold some information that might be helpful. Maybe they would offer information that would lead me more quickly and efficiently to something of benefit to my dad. Or maybe I was spinning my wheels and trudging through all of this and I didn't need to.

"Dad, have you ever thought about sending for your military records?" I asked.

"No," he said. "There wouldn't be anything in them."

"You never know," I said.

"You don't understand."

He hesitated, looking out the window at the morning traffic, which in Walla Walla meant a line of three or four cars in succession. His eyes scanned the horizon. He pulled a handkerchief from his pants pocket and slowly cleaned his glasses. He put them back on and again looked out the window.

"In one of those instructional sessions on Oahu, we were told we'd be traveling with no orders. See, usually whenever you went out to sea, you went with a manila envelope which had your orders in it. That's how they kept track of who was sent where and what they did. But when our group was put aboard that amphibious plane at Ford Island, there were no such orders. So I know there aren't any records of what I did."

He looked down at his hands.

"It's like I was never there," he added.

I didn't know what to say. Of course he was there. I knew the kind of mind he had. I knew he couldn't have made this up or been mistaken. Still, a lack of firm acknowledgment seemed to be eating away at him.

"Anyway," he said interrupting my thoughts. "We were transferred at sea to a submarine. We never saw a name or number but were told it would be the *Sailfish*. That particular submarine had become famous because it was originally the *Squalus* which was re-commissioned the *Sailfish* after a terrible accident at sea. I looked it up the other day on the Internet. It's amazing the information you can get now. I looked up all of the patrols. And there weren't any that went to Iwo Jima. So I just don't know. All this makes me feel like I must be crazy or something. All these years, I believed I was on the *Sailfish*. And it turns out I wasn't. Maybe they just told us that. Or maybe I imagined it all."

He squinted as he looked out the window again.

"Dad," I said. "You didn't imagine it. There has to be documentation of what you did. I think you should send for your records. So tell me…" I said, changing the subject slightly. This time I knew exactly what I was doing. Months ago, he'd left off with he and his comrades boarding a ship in the middle of the ocean. If he was having nightmares recently, my mother hadn't noticed them. And his emotions had returned to an even kilter. And since he seemed open today in a way I hadn't seen in a while, I decided to push forward.

"What was it like once you got on the submarine at Iwo Jima?"

He didn't hesitate in answering. In fact, when he began speaking, he seemed to gain resolve to remember what he had to tell me. When he started to talk, I could hear determination in his voice. He wanted to remember. He wanted to share.

"Well," he said, "I can't exactly remember when we boarded but it was before the initial invasion on February 19. Our sub sat on the bottom of the ocean and shot up an antenna that was attached to the top of the sub. We called it 'the football' because it was shaped like one. It was a top-secret thing at the time. See, usually you had to surface to receive messages but with this thing, most of it stayed below the water. The only part that was above water was an antenna, which of course couldn't be seen by the enemy. If you just picture this vast ocean with a little antenna, you can see why. Anyway, we just sat there copying code day and night. The code could only be copied a short distance, or line of sight. But if you were on a high point or across an uninterrupted surface, that could be extended a couple hundred miles. I suspect we were copying stuff from Chichi-Jima, but I don't really know."

"Did you ever decode things that were really critical?" I asked.

"No. Probably not," he said. "I saw a lot of the decoded messages and they related to supplies and personnel being moved by the Japanese. We just never knew what was important and what wasn't. We just passed the messages on to the cryptanalysts and they figured it all out. But I did get to where I could read what I was copying. And sometimes I read it but mostly there just wasn't time. And we did surface a bit too. The one I remember most vividly was when we surfaced and I could hear cheering. I made my way to the deck of the sub and off to my right I could see the American flag. It was erected on Mount Suribachi. It was quite a sight but, of course, we didn't know how famous that moment would be."

"So you were there when the flag was erected?" I asked, shocked. "That's amazing, Dad!"

"Yeah, I was thinking about it the other day and wondering if I'd seen the first or second flag. You know, they put up the first one and then replaced it with a bigger one a while later," he said.

"Yeah, I remember reading about that," I replied.

"I must have seen the second one," he said. "We were quite a ways out there, so there's no way we would have seen the smaller one. Anyway, a few days after the initial invasion, we were flown back to the base. When we left Oahu, it was virtually deserted. But when we returned, the men were coming back in large groups."

So he had been there! It slipped out so easily, so quickly. He didn't even seem to know that he'd told me something I hadn't known before.

My father had been *in* the war, despite all the times he'd said he hadn't. The stories he'd told when I was a little girl were a very small and very censored part of his experience during WWII. He'd been on a submarine during one of the most important battles of the war.

I tried to fathom what he'd just revealed. The ripples of this one revelation reached so far that I couldn't even think about it all at once. He'd been copying a top-secret Japanese code—at the bottom of the ocean. My father was more than just a sailor who'd sat behind a desk during the war. He and his team had played a very important part in it. My mind spun with the possibilities of what might have happened to him. He'd kept this information hidden for so long. Why? And if he'd successfully kept *this* a secret for more than fifty years, what more might there be?

My father seemed content with the story he'd shared, oblivious to the fact that it had opened up a ton of new questions for me. He took another sip of his water, and then slid across the booth to leave. He handed me the check and a $20 bill.

"I'll meet you at the car," he said.

As I pulled into his driveway, I tried one more time.

"Dad," I said. "You have to send for your records."

This time he didn't argue.

March 6, 1945

Dear Folks,

It's not mail time yet so no new mail since yesterday.

A mob of new guys came in last night and chow line is about a mile long. Also the show is packed so I'll have to get there early.

Had to be a messenger for three hours one afternoon a couple of days ago. That's the only work I've done so far. And didn't do a thing then except wait for something to turn up. Just before quitting, one of the officers sent me for his hat—such a war. Rest of time I read a railroad magazine and studied for my course.

After watching that marimba player Sunday, I've about decided that's for me. They are a little hard to put in your pocket tho.

You know I'm sure glad I don't get letters like most of the guys do. I've seen a lot of them off and on. Jonesy's wife is always way down in the dumps and the letters are so sad that it almost even makes me want to cry too. Don't see how he could stand them. Guess they are better than nothing tho and maybe he even enjoyed them. Think I got the best assortment of mail of any one in the Navy.

All the immediate family—you, Ray & Iris always give me the latest good or bad—in such a way that it's always fun to read 'em over and over. And you should see Kenny & Lois's. She writes one paragraph & he the next always arguing. I really get a kick out of them instead of missing everyone so much. Don't believe I have anyone that writes sad or dry letters. That's sure something I can be thankful for.

By some freak of radio waves—I can pick up Honolulu main police station on one end of band on my radio. When nothing interesting is on the two stations I just tune it over there and get the latest on stolen cars and bad men in general.

Well, nothing to answer so guess I'll close.

Write. Love, Murray

Two weeks after the most harrowing and exciting experience of his life, my father's letters revealed nothing. I was still looking for something, anything, that he'd snuck past censors to confirm what he was now remembering. But there was nothing—not one word.

CHAPTER SIXTEEN

Katakana

We saw the university campus too. It was really nice—lots of grass, which was something neat to see. Camp is all just dirt and tents.
—February 9, 1945

The covered parking at Mr. Ed's, a leftover from its A&W car-service days, was half full. Dad had started using a cane on and off. But even with age finally catching up to him, he never failed to pull the heavy door open for me or anyone else coming or going. We followed the same routine each week. Routine was comforting, I'd decided—it was something my father had realized long ago.

We sat at our favorite table, a booth next to the gas fireplace that was rarely going.

"Dad," I said before our breakfast was served. "Can you explain exactly how you broke the Katakana code?"

"Well, sure," he said without thinking. "Well, at least, I *think* I can."

He'd hesitated for just a moment—long enough for me to predict that he was going to say he didn't remember. But my prediction was wrong.

He unwrapped the paper ring around his napkin, then he folded the napkin carefully into a triangle next to his paper placemat. He lined up his silverware on the napkin, using the tips of his fingers to make the line perfect. I watched quietly as he took the four-color ink pen from his shirt pocket and began drawing letters and symbols on the placemat. His explanation quickly went over my head. But after many questions, he was able to explain it in a way I could understand—at least on a basic level.

In the small communications room aboard the submarine, my father sat at a desk with a Teletype in front of him and earphones on. His job was to *copy* the code, which meant that he listened and then typed. The Japanese language could be heard coming across in a form of Morse code. It was heard in pairs of letters and then a space and then another pair of letters. A combination would come in and my father would simply type the letters he heard. He got so that he could copy and type the code pretty fast. And in fact, to most people the code would have sounded like a very fast drumroll, with no distinguishable differences. But to someone who was trained, it sounded entirely different. Next, a long, thin strip of paper with small holes punched in it came out of an adapted Teletype machine. He would feed the paper into the machine of the cryptanalyst who sat next to him.

"And then, miraculously," he added, "English would come out of the cryptanalyst's machine. I was so close that I could lean over and see what it said. Sometimes it was about the movement of troops, but mostly it was about the movement of supplies."

"But even the movement of troops could be critical, right?" I asked.

"I suppose so," he said. "If a message said they were sending ten thousand Japanese troops to a certain island, that meant they were gearing up for battle. But we never knew what was important and what wasn't. We just passed it on to our superior and he made those decisions."

He thought for a bit, while he clicked his pen, adding details to his drawing in blue, red, green, and black.

"Even something as mundane as sending two thousand cans of beans, though, could mean something to someone who knew what to look for," he said. "Like maybe it meant that a lot of troops were holed up in a certain place. Or maybe our guys knew that beans actually meant something else. I don't know. It boggles the mind to think of all the ramifications. But we didn't have to think of any of that. We just did our job."

As I listened to my father, asked questions, and then listened some more, I realized that he simply did what he was trained to do. He didn't try to analyze it. That wasn't his job. He didn't try to figure out what happened to the data he copied. And he didn't try to figure out what his small part was in this enormous system. That would come many years later. But during the war, he just did as he was told.

What struck me even more so was that all of these years later, he seemed to be considering the importance of what he'd done during the war for the first time in his life. He had opened himself up enough to finally consider that what he did wasn't just a job—it was critical. And yet, because of the secrecy he'd been sworn to, it was unsung. He'd sworn his oath of secrecy five decades ago, and by doing so, he'd silently agreed to never be recognized for what he did. My father and his team had gone their entire lives without a single person thanking them or recognizing them for their heroic contribution to the war.

My father was currently in his eighties. The rest of his team would now be that age too. I was suddenly hit by the realization that it was possible, even probable, that he was the sole survivor. His comrades may have all died by now—without any recognition for their wartime heroism. I hoped I could somehow change that for my father.

As I continued to read his letters, I could see a pattern that began during the war and continued to this day. My father had come back from Iwo Jima to Hawaii. He stepped off of the ship and somehow was able to put it all behind him. He compartmentalized the code breaking, leaving it with those who could be trusted. His letters highlighted this. He went back to Waikiki and to the life of every other sailor.

On liberty, he ate his way through Waikiki: ice cream, cheese sandwiches, chocolate cake, and even lobster. He wandered through town amongst his fellow servicemen, never speaking a word about what he really did.

March 12, 1945

Dear Folks,

Had a nice time yesterday but didn't seem to enjoy it as much as last Sunday for some reason. The newness wore off I 'spose.

Didn't get in town until about 10 and had a dish of ice cream & a cheese sandwich at U.S.O. then caught a station wagon out to the Methodist church and arrived a little late. Sat way up in the galley. Enjoyed it all tho, especially the choir (with civilians). I'm enclosing the program.

After that walked back to town in kind of a roundabout way thru a residential district. Enjoyed that too, as it was away from the hustle & bustle of the city itself. Then got a cab out to Waikiki and ate lunch at my favorite joint. Had lobster salad, iced tea and chocolate cake & ice cream. Then wandered around the Royal Hawaiian Hotel for a while & then caught a cab back to the main U.S.O. in Honolulu again.

Of course couldn't get any mail yesterday so should have about 5 letters and the Chronicle Dispatch *today. Have an hour yet to mail call time—I can hardly wait. It's going to be terrible if I get aboard a ship and get mail only once a week or month or something. Then I'll begin to appreciate the fast service I'm getting now. It will be the same your way too—so don't be surprised if you don't get any for two weeks or so. I'll write often anyway—but then I'm not gone yet. Should get my glasses for sure this Friday and from then on no one knows what. Probably hang around to try 'em out and if they're no good start all over. Personally it's OK with me.*

Well, haven't read any good books or anything so dunno what else to gab about.

The radio is really a life-saver. We get really good programs all the time. Since I got my fonograph I hardly ever listen to any of the programs. Now I'm catching up again.

Also the foto album is swell company. Say, if you can—I mean if materials are still available—wish you would go thru some of those old negatives and find some I don't have and have them printed & send to me. Pictures are almost next to being home even if they are old ones.

S'long for now. Write. Love, Murray

My father was back to his usual life. He walked around the base and around town, and nobody around him knew a thing.

But he wasn't the carefree sailor he'd been before. As he would tell me, the words of the sergeant often came to mind. No matter where he went, he knew that someone could be there to spy on him, watching to see if he'd reveal the military secrets he'd sworn to keep. And so he kept silent, and slowly began to bury the memories of what he'd done.

CHAPTER SEVENTEEN

Women Folk

All my old gal friends are pitching in and really writing nice letters. They'll probably all be lined up at the depot and make me take my choice when I get back.
—May 31, 1945

In his letters, my father often talked about the work his mother and other women were doing. They planted Victory Gardens and viewed the rationing of things like coffee, butter, and sugar, as their patriotic duty. My aunt Iris shared a story with me that exemplified just how deeply held patriotism was, even to the everyday citizen. She remembers her sacrifice of not wearing pantyhose, since nylon was needed for the war effort. The nylons that were fashionable back then had a seam that ran up the back of the leg. Without nylons to wear, Iris and her girlfriends came up with an ingenious solution: they took turns using a dark pencil to draw the line on each other's legs, giving the look of nylons without wearing them.

There has been no generation quite like theirs. World War II pulled our country together in a way that may never be seen again. It was the good that came from the bad. I found numerous Internet sites that had nothing but page after page of information on what women did during WWII. The most famous, of course, was Rosy the Riveter, who exemplified that women could be strong and do the jobs of men. In communities all over the United States, women stepped in wherever they were needed.

Regardless, my father remains old fashioned when it comes to women. He holds the door open for women. He offers women his seat and, even in his eighties, he feels guilty if there's a pregnant woman in the room and he is sitting in one of the few seats.

The attitude toward women in his letters made me laugh. It was such a different time. I just had to hear more. So I shot off a quick email to my father with seven little words, "Tell me about women during the war." The following Wednesday, it was the topic of our conversation.

My Grandma Ruby, he told me, went to work at the railroad for her part during the war. My grandfather had worked for the Northern Pacific Railroad as an agent-telegrapher for years. So, when jobs there were suddenly left open, my grandmother went to work. It was a brand new role for her but she learned fast. She took over the bookkeeping. She taught herself to type and do the shipping and bookwork for the station. My father was clearly proud of his mother's efforts—a bit baffled that she could actually do it, but proud nonetheless.

My father too had worked for the Northern Pacific Railroad before he left for boot camp. Much to his chagrin, he even had to train his replacement. Her name was Ruth. He recalls that she seemed to feel as lost about taking over as a telegrapher as he did about going off to war. While still in training, he was close enough to leave the base on weekends. He used his time to go home to Helix to check on how she was doing. Things were always in a shambles which infuriated him and pleased him all at the same time.

March 15, 1945

Dear Folks,

I still just count the hours until mail time.

Say mom you sure are going to town on your typing—I suppose it's just old stuff now. When you get so you don't try yourself out on a speed test every hour or so, you're an old hand at it.

Gerry, keep away from my glove compartment. That's the place everyone who rode with me used to grab for when they first got in the car. That's where my assortment of grand pianos and drums were kept. If they could get that locked first everyone breathed a sigh of relief and settled down to a pleasant trip with no music.

Sure doesn't seem to me like it's almost five years since I got out of High School but then again, a couple of years at Helix and almost one in the Navy. One nice thing about it is my seniority still going on. Have three years & four months in five more days (As usual I can figure out an anniversary out of almost everything).

I don't think Ruth is doing much of a job of bookkeeping in Helix. She really had a mess when I was there and didn't know what to do next. She'll just let things ride until an auditor begins to get a lot of complaints and tries to straighten her out. You know, things can ride for a long time down there and get in quite a tangle before any one discovers it. If I go back to Helix, I'm going to look things over first and if they aren't in pretty good shape to start with, I'll send for an auditor to clean things up so I can at least have a good start.

I was a little afraid the new seats would be left pretty large for the Fiat but as long as they are comfortable I guess it's OK.

Ought to be really swell for two people or even three now. Maybe you could rig up some "jump" seats in back to fold into the sides in back so you could haul a little coal or a bale of hay around. Sure would give a lot to be working on it. I think it's the ideal rig to tinker with. Not as big and heavy as a standard size car so one man can handle everything pretty well. By the way, what did the seats cost you—or is it a military secret?

You guys will be mechanics yet. Necessity is the mother of invention you know. My start was having an old wreck (more than one) and no dough to hire the repairing done.

Write. Love, Murray

March 20, 1945

Dear Folks,

Really got a letter this time—from all three of you, and just to show how welcome even newspaper clippings are from home—I even read all that's readable on the back side of them in hopes of picking up a little more stray information. Any time you're in the mood I'd enjoy a Walla Walla or Spokane paper.

A dark cloud about an inch square just drifted over so of course it's pouring rain now with the sun shining on all sides. This is a country I'd defy anyone to guess the weather in. About all you can predict safely is that there will be no snow. Suppose you folks must be having a little snow now and then. Sure would like to get my hands in some—although I've probably gone as long before this without seeing any.

And is the Fiat seat as soft as the Chev? That's all I'm worried about. If so then you can just finish the old Chev I guess. Sure hope they send the parts a bit quicker this time from New York but then after all it really hasn't been too long since you actually got the car to Dayton so I guess it's not too bad. Sure seems like a lot longer than just a bit over three months ago that I was wandering around the living room trying to find something to do.

I'll probably wire you guys & gals for a couple thousand when I hit the states for a new car to drive home in. You know how hard it is to get personal checks cashed in a strange town.

I think you should raise the roof about having to do any janitor work mom. That's definitely agents work only—at least that's what I was told. The section crew only works when some of the officials are there in person.

I'll see what I can find in the way of t-shirts with Hula girls. Think it can be arranged. I don't know the population of Honolulu but think about double Spokane.

Boy—the war news is sure coming in thick and fast this morning. Of course the Atlantic side doesn't interest us much except to get the men over here to help end it quicker on this front. Sure good news on every side tho.

By the way, all I see out of my tent is another tent and miles of them beyond. If I raise my eyes a little I can take in the mountains but no ocean. Look right across the bay.

Write. Love, Murray

Once he was in the Pacific, my father wondered and worried about how the railroad station, and in particular his office, would look when he got back. But looking back now, he admits that his biggest fear was that Ruth would do such a great job that he wouldn't have a job to come home to after the war.

CHAPTER EIGHTEEN

Church

The First Methodist Church

Minister
Roy L. Ruth

Beretania & Victoria Sts.
Honolulu, T. H.

Organist-Director
Mary B. Tinker

MORNING WORSHIP

March 3, 1946, Ten Forty-five o'clock

"Let us be silent that we may hear the voice of God."

PRELUDE — "Prelude in D Flat" .... *Chopin*

INVOCATION — "Teach Me, O Lord" .... *Broome*

*HYMN — "Love Divine, All Loves Excelling" .... *No. 372*

PRAYER OF CONFESSION (To be said by all)

Almighty and eternal God, who searchest the hearts of men; we acknowledge and confess that we have not loved thee with all our heart and soul, with all our mind and strength; and that we have not loved our neighbor as ourselves. Forgive us our transgressions, and help us to amend our ways, so that we may henceforth walk in the way of thy commandments, and do those things which are worthy in thy sight; through Jesus Christ our Lord. Amen.

SILENT MEDITATION † † THE LORD'S PRAYER

CHORAL RESPONSE — "Hear Our Prayer, O Lord" .... *No. 596*

• • •

Caught a station wagon out to the Methodist church and arrived a little late…Enjoyed it all tho, especially the choir (with civilians). I'm enclosing the program.—March 12, 1945

Church was the center of our lives when I was growing up. So you wouldn't think it would come as a surprise that my father often referenced church in his letters and even sent home church bulletins. But it *did* surprise me. It just seemed that things like going to church wouldn't have a place for someone in the middle of a war. But then again, church wasn't just a religious experience in my family. It was so much more.

As a child, church was about waking up on any given Sunday and knowing the day was set apart. We girls were dressed in our Sunday best: dresses that tied into a big bow in the back, with matching socks or thick leotards depending on the weather. We wore black or white patent leather shoes depending on the season, and ribbons and bows in our blonde hair. Dad wore a suit, mom a dress. We sat in the fifth pew from the front, all lined up like dolls in a doll house.

I took comfort in the directions: stand up here, speak in unison there, and sing hymn 545 there. My favorite part of the ritual was reading along in the bulletin. I guess one could say I was bored and figured out something to do with my time. But I think that perhaps I am like my father that way. I like order.

I like things lined up and making sense. I like to know what is coming next.

During wartime, the routine of dressing the part, singing the hymns, and hearing the word of God spoken by a man of God must have brought comfort to my father. There was comfort in predictability. But for him, it was even more than that. Our family is, in fact, linked to the founder of the Methodist church, John Wesley.

My great-great-great grandfather, Richard Bunt, was a dear friend to John Wesley in the late 1700s in England. Wesley even stayed in his home a number of times. After my Uncle Raymond traced the family tree and learned this, my father took over, and through a lot of correspondence, finally got a copy of a letter sent from Wesley to my great-great-great grandfather. A framed copy hung on the wall of my parents' living room for years. So the linkage went way back, which was something of pride particularly for my father.

My parents were married in the Methodist church. They made their home in Walla Walla, Washington, just a few highway miles from Dayton. My father built our family home, one he still lives in today. He likes to say he built it "a board a paycheck." The church, like our home, was the framework to which much more was added.

Church was not just a place to go on Sundays from eleven to noon; it was where our friends were. It was where longtime members had children, grandchildren, and great-grandchildren who were raised together. The Klickers and Clizers were just a few of the family names that spanned generations in Pioneer United Methodist church. We went to Sunday school together. We enjoyed potlucks together after church. The Klickers were farmers and donated strawberries for shortcake in the summer and Christmas trees in December to adorn the stage around the pulpit. When we got to junior high, there was an active youth group. When the annual youth-group snow retreat moved up on the calendar, the friends that I'd begged, bribed, and even guilt-tripped into going to church with me were suddenly very interested in it.

Our family never missed a Sunday. Even on our five-week vacations to the Oregon Coast, my parents found a church to attend on Sundays.

April 3, 1945

Dear Folks,

Went to Honolulu as usual Sunday—arrived early and got some breakfast and a haircut. Then went out to church and it was jammed with a crowd out on the side walks. I was pretty early too. So of all days—I never got to church at all on Easter Sunday. Got the usual steak later and wandered all over the library of Hawaii for a few hours.

A couple of new guys around, in and back out again (my tent) all of them left today but then draft was canceled so they came back for the night.

I'm behind fourteen letters now. To fourteen separate people—that's what I get for taking a three day vacation. Got 'em from everyone in the country.

Love, Murray

Though the Methodist genes are on my father's side, it is my mother who can often be found with a Bible in her lap. She joins Bible studies. She studies and applies ancient words written two thousand years ago to her everyday life. But my father is different. In fact, I don't remember ever seeing my dad read the Bible.

"Have you ever read the whole Bible?" I asked one day.

"Well, of course," he answered.

"Really?"

"Sure," he said. "I've read the whole thing."

"Wow," I said. I was truly impressed. "The whole thing, huh? That's impressive. *I* can't even say that. I get hung up on the Old Testament—all those thees and thous and begots. So what's your favorite book of the Bible?" I asked.

"Oh, I don't know. That was a long time ago," he said. "I read it when I was in the service."

"The whole thing?" I asked.

"Yep," he said. "Cover to cover. So now I can say I've read the whole Bible." He laughed.

Leave it to my methodical father, I thought, to read the Bible from Genesis to Revelation while in the midst of a war.

CHAPTER NINETEEN

Breakdown

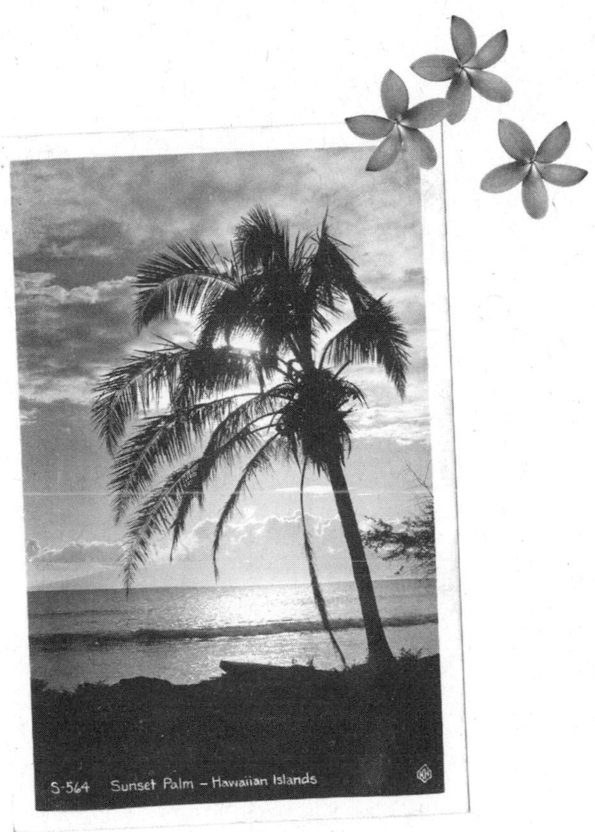

But it's just like another dream—off that darned ship and on this plane. We have everything around us here you ever read or heard about the islands.—January 9, 1945

It was another hectic night at our house, but we'd managed to get the dinner dishes loaded into the dishwasher and the older kids had finished their homework. Caleb, who had never been interested in television, was playing not so quietly with his matchbox cars on the floor. We'd just settled in to watch *America's Funniest Home Videos* when the phone rang.

"It's your mom," Ric said handing me the phone.

"Hi, Mom," I said.

"Your dad has had some kind of a breakdown," she blurted out.

My heart sank. I put my hand over my stomach as nerves invaded. I had a sick feeling as I took the phone to my bedroom, not even bothering to turn the lights on. I stood next to the bed unable to move any further.

"Is he OK?" I asked.

She didn't answer my question.

"We had just parked at the grocery store. We were sitting in the car," she continued. "I had been talking about my concern for a dear friend. I was just worried about her and I started telling him about her problem. But then I realized that she had trusted me and I shouldn't have told him."

"Now, Murray," my mother had said, "you understand you can't talk to anyone else about this. You can't tell anyone. This is a secret."

"Secret!" he shouted, startling her. "You don't think I can keep a secret? I've been keeping a secret for fifty-seven years."

My mother was stunned. Somehow, what had started as a typical trip to the grocery store had turned into something else. In their fifty years of marriage, she'd never seen him like this before. My father didn't yell, ever. But this day one moment he was fine, the next he was screaming at her. She simply couldn't fathom how fast and furious he had changed.

And then he did something else he never did—he cried. My father, who wasn't a crier, began to sob like a baby. And as his anger dissolved to tears, he told her about the day that changed him forever.

In the waters off of Okinawa, on the deck of a ship, my father and his friend Mal sat across from each other on rolling chairs. Kamikazes littered the sky as my dad and Mal went about their work, copying the Japanese code. Every ten minutes or so they rolled their chairs across the deck of the ship to exchange places. After one of these exchanges, Dad had just buckled back in place when a kamikaze hit the water close by and shrapnel flew. In the chaos that followed, he turned to his friend.

Mal had been wounded by shrapnel. My father went to him. He cradled him like a baby. He held his dying friend in his arms. "Oh, Murray" were Mal's last words. In the mind-numbing scene that followed, he couldn't let go of his friend. He couldn't leave him. His hands clenched tight to him until a comrade pried them open. The next thing he knew he was waking up in a military hospital some time later. This was the secret he kept.

I was stunned. I felt a wave of indescribable emotions. I was sad that he'd bore this secret all by himself. He'd kept it inside until it hurt so bad that it had to get out. I'd been talking to him about the war for such a long time now. My feeling that there was something more to his story turned out to be right. But before my mind traveled down that path, I was hit with an overwhelming sense of guilt.

Did I cause this? I wondered. Did all my prying and questioning cause him to have a breakdown? Did I bring to the surface something so painful that it had remained untold for more than fifty years? Maybe it should have remained untold. Maybe it was never *meant* to be brought to the surface. My father was in unimaginable pain. Was it my fault?

Before getting off the phone, Mom and I agreed that I would wait for him to tell me about it. It was too important to simply treat it like any other message to pass on. Hopefully, in time, my father would feel safe enough to tell me his secrets too.

Later that night, I lay in bed going over what my mother had shared. I ran it through my mind several times before I realized what she had said. She'd said Okinawa, not Iwo Jima. How could that be? My father had told me about Iwo Jima. But he'd never even mentioned Okinawa. I didn't know much about Okinawa, but what I did know was that it was a big deal during the war. Since Dad didn't know that I knew, I couldn't ask him about it. And even if he did know, what would I say? What could I possibly say to make it better?

The following day, after work, I went to the shelf where I kept the original notebooks. I ran a finger along the spine of the blue and gray notebooks. But I didn't take them down. I couldn't. Not anymore. I left the notebooks where they belonged. I left them where this whole journey had started: on a bookshelf, hidden from everything, hidden from life. Then I slowly lowered myself to my knees. Kneeling beside my bed, my face buried in a blanket, I sobbed. Not even realizing that I was in a prayer position, I cried out.

"Why?" I whispered at first. "Why?" I said louder. "Why did he have to remember this? Why? Why couldn't he live out his last years in peace? Why couldn't it have stayed buried?"

It wasn't a prayer. I was too angry, too disillusioned, to pray. My hands weren't folded and my heart was not petitioning. God allowed this to happen. He allowed it all. He made my father have this terrible experience and then he brought the memory crashing down on him when he was so frail. It wasn't fair and I was mad at God for letting it happen.

My father and I continued to go to breakfast on Wednesdays, and I still stopped by occasionally, but I didn't bring anything with me. We didn't talk about the war. He had changed. Every now and then I could see it in his eyes. He'd bow his head or stare out the window a little too long. And I knew. He remembered. He sat in quiet grief and all I could do was watch.

My mother too saw the quiet grief. Her concern prompted her

to ask the impossible of him. She asked him to talk about what had happened to someone other than family. Ed Hamshar was their minister, and Nila his wife. Much to my mother's surprise, he agreed. They met at the minister's home.

My father told his whole WWII story, from beginning to end. My father, a man of few words, talked nonstop for two hours. During that time, the Hamshars didn't interrupt or even ask questions. They simply let him talk. My mother prayed, and she knew the Hamshars were praying too.

As they got ready to leave, Nila said she had a word for my father.

"I feel like I'm supposed to tell you that you are not crazy," she said.

When they got in the car to go home, my father said that those words meant a lot to him. He said he often felt like he was crazy. But her words brought a measure of peace to him.

Talking to someone about his experience and his grief was a first step on a path that I hoped would lead him back to me. I had started this and I wanted to help make it better, if that was even possible. But for now, all I could do was wait and hope.

A few weeks later, I went to my parents' house when I knew my father wouldn't be home. Mom greeted me with a cup of tea and a tin of shortbread cookies.

"I was going to call you today," she said. "Your dad said to tell you girls about his friend, about his breakdown in the parking lot."

"Mom," I said after a few nibbles of cookie. "Do you think

this happened because of me, I mean because of the letters and me asking all those questions? Is it my fault?" I choked back tears and tried to keep my voice from shaking.

"Probably," she said gently.

My heart sank.

We sat in quiet for a moment too long. She seemed deep in thought. Finally, she broke the silence.

"But Karen," she added, "this has been coming for a long time. There has always been something about your father. It was like he'd built a wall up around himself. Nobody could get in and he couldn't get out."

She looked out the window.

"I think this is the answer. This is what he's been holding in for all these years." She looked back at me. "This is a new beginning for him. You know I've prayed for your dad for so many years, and I didn't even know what I was praying for. I believe this is an answer to those prayers."

I couldn't speak. I knew my voice would crack and tears would spill.

"Ever since you and your dad started having breakfast together, I've prayed about your time together. I hoped that somehow your time with him would finally bring peace to him. It just seems like he's never had peace."

I didn't know what to say. I finished a few cookies and left before he got back.

CHAPTER TWENTY

Secrets

By the way, all I see out of my tent is another tent and miles of them beyond. If I raise my eyes a little I can take in the mountains but no ocean.—March 20, 1945

I guess your mom told you about my little incident in the parking lot," my father said the next Wednesday.

I nodded.

I didn't know what to say. *I'm sorry?* But sorry for what? Sorry his friend died or sorry he'd remembered? So I didn't say anything.

"I can't believe that after all these years it all came back to me like that," he said. "Like it was happening all over again. Can you believe that?"

I shook my head.

"Mal and I were friends," he said. "We both knew how to copy the Japanese code and we did it side by side at Iwo Jima. Then a few weeks later, we were ordered to write another set of letters. We were sent right back out and did the same thing but this time at Okinawa. But when they went to transfer us to the sub there, the communications room was flooded. So they transferred us to the deck of a ship. The sky was black with kamikazes.

"We were actually kind of goofing off when it happened. We were on the deck of this huge ship. When we were at Iwo Jima we made up a game. Seems strange now, to be fooling around literally in the middle of a war. But that's what we did. There were places all around the perimeter of the deck where we could work. All we needed was a place to clip our rolling chair so we could stay in one place when the ship moved, which was constantly. And there were these metal rings at regular intervals where we could do that. But we didn't work next to each other. We were all the way across the deck from each other.

"Well, just for fun every now and then, we'd wait until the ship rolled so one side was higher than the other, then unclip and roll across the deck to the other side. Within seconds the ship would roll to the other side and the other of us would unclip and roll across to the other side. So we switched places that way. It broke up the monotony and it was kind of fun.

"One day, for some reason, when Mal and I changed places, I got out of my chair. I can't remember exactly why, but sometimes we did that. I was sitting on a wooden crate. Well, right after we'd switched places, a kamikaze hit close and a piece of shrapnel hit right between my legs; it was imbedded into the crate. I instinctively reached down to pull it out and it was hot. It burned my finger."

He opened his hand and looked down at his finger.

"Right there," he said. "It's the darndest thing. See that?"

I looked at his finger to see a half-inch long scar of sorts. Actually it looked more like a tattoo. It was blue and in the shape of an elongated *c*. I remembered it well. When I was a little girl, I would run my tiny fingers across the scars on his hand. But the blue scar was my favorite. It wasn't raised like the others. It was smooth like the rest of his skin.

"You know, a few years ago I tried to get it out," he said. "I took my pocket knife and tried to dig it out."

I cringed.

"And it hurt…a lot," he said with a little laugh. "So I decided to leave it be. So anyway, it was some time after that—maybe hours, maybe days, I just can't remember—that Mal and I were on the deck again. But this time we were in those rolling chairs. We had just changed places when this Kamikaze hit the water close by. For some reason, I looked over at Mal and saw that he'd been hit. I unstrapped and ran over to him. I cradled him like a baby. And Mal looked up at me and said, 'Oh, Murray.'

"Then it's kind of a blur. I remember I was holding on to him so tight that someone, a sergeant or something, ordered someone to get me off of him. They had to pry my fingers away from his shirt one finger at a time. Then I remember standing up and brushing my shirt with my hands trying to get the blood off. It's the craziest thing, right? I was trying to brush blood off with my hands. Then I remember that same sergeant telling someone to take my shirt off of me and they did. The next thing I remember was waking up in Aiea Naval Hospital and seeing a pretty blonde nurse. Anyway, so that's the story."

"I'm sorry you had to go through that," I said, finally finding my words.

"Oh, lots of guys had it way worse than I did," he said. "You know, if Mal and I hadn't switched places, I would have been the one gone and he would be the one with kids and grandkids."

"I'm glad you're here," I said. I didn't know if it was the right thing to say or not.

I went home and took a reference book off the shelf.

"Okinawa," I whispered.

Turning the pages, I learned that the initial invasion began on April 1, 1945. I opened my father's letters and started reading.

Just as before, I looked for clues about what had happened at Okinawa. But this time I wasn't so hopeful. I had come to understand that there would not be neat answers that fit into a box. I read each letter staring with those dated a week before the initial invasion. Since he wasn't there for the initial invasion, I stopped on March 30. That was the time, roughly, that my father was there. But after hours of reading and rereading, the only possible clue I uncovered is the fact that there was a break in the letters. He went just shy of a full week without a single letter. On each end were letters dated March 23 and March 30 that sat as brackets around a blank space.

March 23, 1945

Dear Folks,

Nothing new has been added in the past twenty four hours. One thing—I bought a bottle of pop. That was exactly my doings for the day. Saw the show "Winged Victory" last night. It was really swell. You should see it if you want to see about what we went through to get over here. It's about the A.A.F. but the training was about the same (except for the gold bar when they finished).

We get all the popular programs all right, on the radio but they aren't direct—they are always transcription thru the two local stations. All but one are in excellent English too. They have American (stateside) announcers and it's just exactly the same as listening to KHQ or something, in Spokane.

Write. Love, Murray

March 30, 1945

Dear Folks,

Before I forget—sent a package a couple of days ago first class mail (not air-mail). Inside is one of my amphibious insignias—in case you didn't know. It goes on the left arm sleeve at the top. That's what I'm attached to so I'm entitled to wear it. In the Navy there are just a few branches that wear those special insignia. The Amphibs, Seabees, and P.T. crews, the rest of the service don't wear any specialty designation. Also that overseas bar is all mine too—American theatre and Asiatic Pacific theatre. Everyone here is overseas so you never see any one wearing an overseas ribbon. Thought you might hang 'em on my star in the window or something with that rating badge I sent before just for the novelty of it.

Still have a lot of new guys around. They come and go but I stay on. Will see the doc Monday and got an appointment for eye exam. If no change I'll be set any day after that to catch a draft. If a change is required that will probably mean another month or more. As far as I'm concerned they sure need changing all right.

Go on liberty Sunday and sure hope I arrive in time to go to church and think I'll take in the dinner afterwards this time too.

Write. Love, Murray

As I read, I wondered if these letters were among those written ahead of time and mailed while he was at Okinawa. How strange it seemed that his mother received such a glowing report of her son's wartime experiences while he was going through such a trauma.

But even if the letters themselves didn't reveal anything, did she notice that he didn't write for almost a week? And what about that break? Was that during the time he spent in the hospital? Had he been treated for his wounds—physical and mental?

One thing was certain, physical wounds heal, but the place of pain will always have a scar. Maybe it was the same for emotional wounds. Maybe a place where the pain was at one time unbearable could never be the same, no matter how good it looked or how well-healed it appeared.

CHAPTER TWENTY-ONE

Remembering

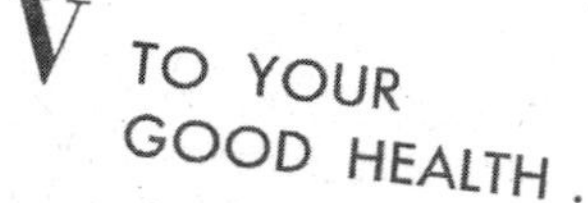

V TO YOUR
GOOD HEALTH . . .
HOSPITALIZATION
MEDICAL CARE
DOMICILIARY CARE
ARTIFICIAL LIMBS
MECHANICAL APPLIANCE AIDS
Hospitalization, Medical and Institutional Care

VETERAN'S
GUIDE
DEPARTMENT OF VETERAN'S AFFAIRS
STATE OF WASHINGTON

Some of the pessimistic ones say, "Golden State in '48—Bread line in '49"—mostly cause it rhymes well I think.
—April 24, 1945

I love the first barbeque of the season," I said.

"Me too!" Caleb shouted.

The smell of barbecue wafted in from the backyard where Ric was cooking. I spread the blue-and-white checkered cloth over the dining table and put a stack of plates at the end. In the kitchen, I started pulling things from the fridge.

"Here," I said handing the kids bowls of chips, salsa, macaroni salad, and condiments.

"Grandma and Grandpa will be here in a few minutes," I said. "And you know Grandpa; he's never late when food is being served."

"Hello?" Dad hollered as he and Mom came through the front door. "Anybody home?"

The kids laughed. I did too.

"I was just saying that you are never late if food is involved," I said.

"Well, that's the truth," my mother said.

Dad was already at the table nibbling on chips when Ric came in from the backyard with hamburgers and hotdogs stacked on a long white serving dish.

"Dinner's served," I announced as the kids swarmed the table.

"Sorry it's not steak, Dad," Ric said glancing at me. "Karen insisted on hamburgers."

"Well, I love a good hamburger," Mom said. "There's nothing better than the first barbequed burger in the spring."

Dad and Ric exchanged glances. They liked their steaks.

After dinner, the boys went out to play while Danielle and Grandma sat on the porch swing. Clearing off the table, I made trips back and forth to the kitchen. I was so focused on getting the food off the dining table before Cocoa decided to make a meal of it that I hadn't noticed Dad. As I pulled the tablecloth off, I saw him.

Instead of following the family outside, he'd made himself comfortable in the living room, sitting in the recliner. Finding a quiet moment in our house was rare. As I moved into the room, he asked a question before I even had a chance to sit down.

"You didn't find any clues in my letters about Okinawa, did you?" Dad asked.

"No," I said.

A few weeks had passed since we'd talked about his breakdown. And to be honest, I'd been avoiding the subject of Okinawa altogether. This time I hadn't told him about rereading the letters surrounding that period of time. I was surprised that he was the one to bring it up. I didn't think he had even thought about it. I was wrong.

"I didn't find anything," I said.

"Your mom said it figured that the first thing I remembered after waking up in the hospital was a pretty blonde nurse," Dad laughed.

I laughed too.

"She doesn't know the half of it," he said in a soft voice. "I remember lots of things. It comes back in bits and pieces."

“Like what?” I asked, taking the pillow beside me and hugging it.

“Well,” he started, “I remember that when I woke up I was in a hospital room. And there was this nurse who was sitting in the corner reading something. I can’t remember if I said something or what, but she looked at me and rushed out into the hallway and called the doctor. The doctor came rushing over to my bed. He asked me if I remembered what I had been doing before coming to the hospital. I told him that I had been copying code on a ship off of Okinawa. The doctor was about to ask another question but these two marines were at the door. They had sidearms, pistols in holsters, and they pulled them out.”

“Oh my gosh,” I said. “Are you kidding me?”

“No. I’m not kidding,” Dad said. “They didn’t wave them around or anything, just kept them pointed at the floor. Anyway, one of them told the doctor that I could not talk about what I’d been doing. The doctor said that he was just trying to see if my mind was okay. So then the doctor took out his stethoscope and started to do a regular exam and they put their guns away. The marines stayed outside my door all the time, but from then on, the doctor only asked me how I felt for the rest of the time I was there.”

He seemed to be thinking, so I didn’t say anything.

“Oh, and my hand was all bandaged up,” he said. “The nurse unwound that ball of gauze ’round and ’round, and when she was done, there were just a bunch of scrapes and scratches. A lot of bandage for nothin’.”

“How long were you in the hospital?” I asked.

He looked down for a bit and then looked around.

“I just don’t know,” he said.

"Do you think it was like a few days or a month?" I asked.

"Probably not as long as a month. I just don't know. Maybe a few days or a week. I just don't know." His frustration was visible now.

"What else do you remember?" I asked.

"Well, I remember that this guy—I can't remember if he was a doctor, or what, but he kept telling me that I wasn't going to remember any of this. He said it over and over, and I felt like he was trying to brainwash me into believing it. It made me try even harder to remember. Then one day someone came to me and said I was going back to the barracks and to my old job. A Navy car came and picked me up. I just went back to a normal life, like nothing had ever happened. I had just started a new job right before I was sent to Okinawa. So I went back to that job."

"Did you ever see the guys you worked with at Okinawa again?" I asked.

"No," he said. "And I didn't care to either. My mind was pretty much blanked out because of what happened to Mal. I was with him when he died. I should have contacted his folks. I should have told them that he didn't die alone. But I never did. I regret that."

He looked out the window.

"Looks like rain," he said.

Just then, Caleb ran in the house.

"Mom," he said excitedly. "There's a storm coming. Come on, come on!"

Caleb jumped up and down and finally pulled me by the hand.

"Come on, Dad," I said. "You get to experience what the Alaniz family does when there's a storm."

I pulled the blankets off the back of the couch and joined the rest of the family outside under the cover of the porch. Snuggled on the porch swing and the wicker chairs, we waited for the pounding rain and silently wished for a show of lightning. Bolts of lightning caressed the blue-gray sky and thunder brought shrieks of awe. Then something caught my eye. It was Dad. He hadn't followed us to the porch. He stood on the other side of the picture window. His eyes were locked on the horizon in the distance. The storm came and went and he never moved.

The letters I was reading now, after he was sent back to base, were so far removed from the trauma he'd experienced. That could mean one of two things: either he was faking every letter, making it sound like everything was great, or his mind had already begun the arduous task of burying what was too painful to bear. I suspected it was the latter.

April 6, 1945

Dear Folks,

I'm an early bird today. I went to breakfast a few minutes ago—for first time in a couple of months. Had soft bacon, scrambled eggs (powdered), and bread with butter and jam, plus coffee & cereal if you want it and figs for dessert. It was all too much for me.

Rain is pouring down now—looks like an all day siege but may let up. What I hate about this rain is that the mud is so bloomin' sticky. Just like glue—you can't shake it off or hardly scrape it off. Guess I'll just stay in today & write & study a bit more. Supposed to muster (roll call) about now but it's raining so hard I expect a "delay muster" call in a minute. If not we'll all float over I guess—it's just outside my tent anyway.

Got paid 36 bucks yesterday. That's about what I usually get—$72 a month clear. Getting my overseas pay now. That's not bad money. Sure can't seem to save any tho. Things are so expensive if you want to do much that it runs into money sometimes on liberty. A cab is usually $1.50 out to Waikiki—of course you can start up on a jammed bus for a dime if you want to stand in line. Then a steak with all the trimmings for a real meal amounts to two bucks—on the other hand for 50 cents you can eat a couple hamburgers and a glass of pineapple juice which is just as filling. All depends on the person—what you spend I guess. Wanted to save enough to have the flivver painted but may yet—I'm still here.

That's all for now. Write.

Love, Murray

April 9, 1945

Dear Folks,

Well I didn't get on liberty today—kind of got changed around in my set-up here. About 20 of us unassigned men got assigned to various jobs around the base just to keep us from loafing too much. My job is helping in the storeroom. That is my permanent job as long as I'm here. And I don't like it. As far as work I don't do any more than I ever did. Can come back to my tent (about half a block away) any time I want to wash clothes or something. But doubt if I'll be able to get off Sundays like before, unless my liberty day just happens to fall on that day. Do have a little better liberty set up. Get out once every six days instead of eight as before. All in all the change doesn't amount to anything—doesn't change my status any as far as future goes. Anyway—now I go on liberty tomorrow. They seem to kind of leave it up to me about my glasses so guess I'll see if can get an appointment again about next Thursday or Friday. Never do today what you can put off 'til tomorrow.

Show tonite is "Dr Wasaill" with Gary Cooper. Think it's kind of gory—may not go. Well a hard days work has made me hungry. Better hunt for the chow line.

Love, Murray

April 11, 1945

Dear Folks,

Well, back from liberty again—which is the only new thing that's happened and ever does happen. Did nothing of importance except got a new pair of shoes in town ($7.35). They are softer than the regular Navy issue and thicker leather sole. A little different design but then it doesn't matter about that and it's a bit of a change at least. Really got in to town in a hurry this time—then of course on Sundays will really have a reason to get there early—things are jammed and I can't get there in time for church ever—still up to my old tricks. I hop on a trolley and ride *to the end of the line and back. Still have a few new ones to see yet. Really can get around the island now. It was sure a mess at first but now I'm practically an old timer.*

Most of the working class natives talk sort of a pidgin English that's hard to understand at first but you get used to it.

You know—one thing that amazes me is the price of houses around here. You never see one advertised in the pages under ten thousand and they run usually around twenty to thirty thousand and many a lot more, and not really nice houses either. I saw one something like yours yesterday (they show pictures quite often) for $18,500!

Hope you start receiving the paper soon if you haven't already. The want ads and local news will tell you a lot that I never think of.

For some unknown reason—they tell me I have a liberty again tomorrow. Every five or six days now. Still haven't done any work. I'm getting my letter writing done on the job. It's a good thing because I'm way behind on the letters and also in my studies. Got a swell book yesterday that you might be interested in Gerry? It's "Your Wings" by Jordanoff. It cost three bucks and tells how to fly with all rules, regulations and air navigation, even parachute jumping—just everything and it's simple too. It has a cartoon or two on nearly every page like Walt Disney's stuff which makes it really interesting. It's a big book—will take quite a while to read it.

I'll send it home for safekeeping when I finish it. Kind of wanted to be prepared just in case.

Write soon. Love, Murray

The job my father went back to after being in the hospital was not difficult. You could hear it in his letters. Was he given such a job because he was fragile? Was someone looking out for him, trying to make things easy on him because he'd had a breakdown after his friend died in his arms? Someone with a mind brilliant enough to break a complicated code probably wasn't expected to break emotionally or mentally. But my father's brilliant mind *had* broken. And so his work in naval intelligence was over.

CHAPTER TWENTY-TWO

Mourning

Oahu, T. H.
April 19, 1945

Dear Folks,

The uppermost thing in all "G.I.'s" minds today is the death of Ernie Pyle. He was more important to the ordinary foot soldier than a general. He seemed to be right in there with them all the time and above all he headed right back into action out here after "serving his time" in the European theatre. Ernie could have stayed home without hurting his reputation or anything. I usually read his columns before the funnies even. They usually say exactly what the enlisted man is thinking all the time.

The uppermost thing in all G.I.'s minds today is the death of Ernie Pyle. He was more important to the ordinary foot soldier than a general.—April 19, 1945

I was a block away from his house when I noticed Dad was sitting on a lawn chair in the front yard. It was Wednesday, our breakfast day, but he'd never been waiting for me like that before. As I got closer, he stood and walked to the curb. He leaned in as I rolled the window down.

"What do you think of my flag?" he asked.

"What flag?" I asked, looking past him.

He was grinning like someone who was keeping a great secret. He motioned for me to follow him. I parked the car.

"Stand right here," he said.

I stood in the grass next to his chair. He went to the garage and returned with a pole about six feet long. Some sort of fabric was held between his arm and his side. His posture was erect, his stride confident, almost a march. He slid the pole into a hole in the ground that I hadn't noticed and wiggled it until it was sturdy.

He unfolded the fabric; it was an American flag. Then he attached it to the pole. With a simple sliding motion, he erected the flag twenty feet in the air. The flagpole proudly displayed the flag. He stood back and looked up at it and then at me.

"It's great!" I said.

My father had always been patriotic. He was always the first one to put up a flag on Memorial Day, Veterans Day, and all of the other flag-raising holidays. During parades he stood and took his hat off when the flag was marched by. So this new addition didn't surprise me.

Each week after, when I arrived, the flag was raised. He followed proper flag etiquette, taking it down at night since it wasn't illuminated. Sometimes, he raised it right when I arrived to pick him up. He loved it when the wind blew *just right* so that the flag was unfurled perfectly.

I loved watching him raise it. There was such pride in every movement he made. When it was clicked into its final position, he'd look up. It was a symbol of strength and somehow he drew strength *from* it.

A few weeks had passed when I stopped to pick him up for breakfast and he was sitting next to the flagpole. He raised himself from the lawn chair, giving it one last glance before getting into the car. I'd driven just a few blocks when he spoke.

"It's for Mal," he said. "The flag. It's for Mal."

It all came together then. He wasn't drawing strength from the flag itself but from what it represented: his fallen friend. And when he sat out there, next to the flagpole, it was his friend's presence that gave him strength.

As we continued on to breakfast, I felt a well of emotions. My father and I had come full circle. At the beginning, I'd felt the need to fill every silence with words, every emotion with explanation. But as we rode together and then ate together, there was no need to do that. We understood each other, and we knew that silence too could be communication.

Over the next few months, I would find him out there, in the lone lawn chair, just sitting, looking up at that flag or watching people walk by his house. When he heard that you could order a flag that had been flown over the White House, he ordered one and replaced the one he had. He knew all of the holidays and occasions that one is supposed to raise the flag, and he made up a few of his own too. He put it up as a celebration of birthdays and out-of-town visits from family. And sometimes he put it up for no apparent reason at all.

What I began to realize, though, was that the flag was more than just a patriotic symbol. It meant that he hadn't forgotten. He'd never been able to go to a funeral or memorial service for Mal. There wasn't a grave to visit. But now, after more than fifty years, he had a place to go to remember.

Mal's death marked the greatest tragedy of my father's young life. It was felt by him and somewhere it was felt by his family. But within a month's time, the whole nation would mourn together. My father put words to that loss in a letter home.

April 13, 1945

Dear Folks,

I was on liberty yesterday and out at a show at Kaimuki when they flashed the news of the presidents death on the screen. Of course everyone read it over a couple of times before believing it. Practically everyone walked out of the theatre kind of dazed. I was among them. Got on a street car heading back for Honolulu.

A big negro top sergeant sat down next to me. Someone in the front of the bus held up an extra of the paper that said "Roosevelt Dies." The negro said "I heard it but I didn't believe it." Tears were streaming down his face. Then as I walked across the street a boy asked me if I know why colors were lowered all over town. News came quick and it was hard to believe. It happened at 11:05 a.m. Hawaiian time.

Spent a couple of hours talking to the lady at the U.S.O. about the proposed ex-railroaders club. We really got off to a flying start. I told her I hardly knew from one day to the next whether I'd be here or not but she said that part was OK. So we mapped out plans for a meeting the 23rd. She insisted that I was a good sign painter so grabbed a ruler and pen etc and made a big multi color notice to put up in the lobby.

Oh yes, if Chad B. arrives, it will probably be right where I am. Hope you can run down his address for me when Mr. Broughton finds out about it.

Glad the Honolulu paper is getting thru to you. Now maybe you'll get some of the local news I never think of.

Everyone is going in for baby kittens for pets now. They are kind of cute when they are little. Have a ma cat and five kittens kind of mottled gray color live where I'm working and at the main office a set of pure black ones.

Have several advantages to my job. I'm temporarily on the staff now so I get a special card that lets me in to the shows without standing in line an hour or so and I get my mail an hour earlier. I don't have to stand "quarters" for half hour every morning listening to a bunch of routine bulletins. A hard working man has advantages all right. By the way—I'm "working" now. Doing nothing as usual. Have a messenger watch this afternoon from four hours. Just drink cokes and gab with the gang.

Well, this letter must end.

Love, Murray

"Do you remember when President Roosevelt died?" I asked.

"Oh yes. I remember it very well," he said.

He proceeded to tell me the story of being at the Kaimuki movie theater and then on the bus. The story he told was identical to the one in his letter.

"I just read about it in one of your letters," I said.

"Really?" he asked. "I wrote about that?"

I nodded.

"You have a fantastic memory, Dad. You told the story almost verbatim," I said.

"I don't know about the good memory. I don't seem to remember anything these days. I get in the car and can't even remember where I'm going," he said.

"Well, that's nothing," I said. "I do that all the time."

He thought for a moment.

"Some things I just remember in detail," he said.

"You know, Mom says you have a photographic memory. She says you always have."

"Oh, I don't have a photographic memory," he replied. "Your mom doesn't know what she's talking about."

I didn't tell him that my sisters and I thought that too. I didn't tell him how different he is. I didn't tell him that it's not normal to read a book in one night and then be able to tell every detail about it decades later. I didn't tell him how unusual it is that he easily understands complex schemes and commits them to memory, apparently without even realizing it. My father is the smartest man I've ever known. And yet when it came to emotions, it was a different story.

What does it take for a man who remembers everything to forget? His best friend dying in his arms? As I read the letters dated late April, I could see an accumulation of events that were added to the death of his friend. Were they part of what drove him to bury it all away?

April 19, 1945

Dear Folks,

The uppermost thing in all G.I.'s minds today is the death of Ernie Pyle. He was more important to the ordinary foot soldier than a general. He seemed to be right in there with them all the time and above all, he headed right back into action out here after "serving his time" in the European Theatre. Ernie could have stayed home without hurting his reputation or anything. I usually read his columns before the funnies even. They usually say exactly what the enlisted man is thinking all the time.

Didn't do anything unusual but eat ice cream—and that's not unusual. Got a hair cut but forgot to tell them to shave the cookie duster off. Too bad. Maybe next year.

I was the messenger this morning and got to write letter this afternoon. Guess I'll have to brush up on my code and typing a bit too as I get speed tests in those subjects. It's getting more complicated.

I hardly even knew who was vice president let alone where he was from. Of course now we know we are in good hands. He can probably do a little drinking and get us out of the national debt or something. Still seems hard to believe F.D.R. isn't at the helm.

Wish you could get a picture of the Fiat with the first door open and the family or at least part of it—gathered 'round.

That's all there is—there is no more.

Write. Love, Murray

Dad rode over to my house on his Segway. We sat on the front porch, talking about nothing. Then I remembered Ernie Pyle.

"Who was Ernie Pyle?" I asked.

"You don't know who Ernie Pyle was?" he replied.

He was dumbfounded.

"Well, Ernie Pyle was probably the best news reporter who ever lived. You know, nowadays we see all this news from what they call imbedded reporters. You know what that means, right?"

"Yeah," I said. "The reporters who go right along with the troops."

"Right up to the front lines," he said. "Ernie Pyle did that during WWII. He went with the soldiers right up to the front lines. And in the end it cost him his life. He was shot by a sniper. The GIs probably mourned him more than they did Roosevelt. He was just one of the guys. He told the stories in a way that everyone could understand from the guys themselves to the housewife at home. Anyway, he was a hero to us."

Too much was happening at once in his letters. I felt overwhelmed and I wondered if that's how he felt when he was going through it. First he'd lost his friend, then news of President Roosevelt's death, and finally Ernie Pyle's. When he talked about Ernie Pyle, it was like he was talking about the death of a friend. I wondered what it felt like to him back then. Did he feel like the world was falling apart, every foundation ripped away? Perhaps that's why he kept his memories in a secure place for more than fifty years. Did one thing stack on another until he couldn't take it anymore?

It is said that people don't commit suicide over one thing; it's always a number of things, the accumulation of which becomes unbearable. I wondered if my father's mind simply knew how much he could take and built a wall to save him. With the wall's foundations firmly planted, even before he returned home, he could go on living. Had his life been spared by his mind's ability to do this? It was impossible to even consider the alternative.

CHAPTER TWENTY-THREE

Lost Time

Personally I would be glad to be turned loose over here in the middle of a pineapple field with orders to find my way back to Dayton.—May 31, 1945

Dad and I continued to meet every Wednesday for eggs Benedict. However, since the day he remembered Mal, our time together had changed. Before, I had charged ahead with questions. But now I watched him for clues. I learned that his grief was almost imperceptible—the turn of his lip, the tip of his brow. If I saw any of those signs, I didn't ask any questions. Sometimes we went for weeks at a time without talking about the war at all.

But then there were times when his demeanor changed. There was a bounce to his step and a sparkle in his eyes. It was those times that we talked the most.

"You know what bothers me the most?" he asked one Wednesday. "That time I lost."

"What time?" I asked.

"After that time on the ship, when, you know…" he said. "After…"

"After Mal died?" I asked.

He nodded.

"I woke up in Aiea Naval Hospital. But I don't know how I got there," he said. "They must have flown me but I don't remember."

A bell above the door jangled. He watched as a young family came in. He kept watching them as he continued.

"I lay there at night when I can't sleep. I just go through it over and over in my head. How did I get to the hospital? Who was there? It's driving me crazy. You know I can remember every moment of my life except this one. Why can't I remember?" he asked.

He was looking me in the eye now. His eyes were pleading, asking me to figure this out for him. But I didn't have the answer.

"I don't know," I said. "What's the last thing you do remember?"

"I just remember trying to wipe the blood off of my shirt with my hands. I was just brushing my shirt like this," he said. He brushed his hands down the front of his shirt.

I couldn't help picturing it in my mind's eye, blood saturating his white shirt. The horror he must have felt when, with every swipe, more blood was transferred to his hands. The more he tried to erase it, the more bloodied he became.

I drew in a silent breath.

"And then what?" I asked.

"Then someone said, 'Somebody get that shirt off of him,'" he remembered. "And a couple of sailors pulled it over my head. And that's all I remember."

"Until the pretty blonde nurse," I added, trying to lighten the mood. He smiled a little.

"I just wonder if it's in there," he said tapping his head. "I was probably on an airplane. It had to take eight or nine hours to get there. What did I do? Did I talk? Did someone talk to me? I must have just been out of my mind."

"You were traumatized," I said.

"When I woke up in the hospital, I asked that nurse if I was hurt. She said some people get hurt in their bodies and some people are hurt up here." He tapped his head again. "I was probably in the psych ward and didn't even know it. I got an email from your sister the other day and she said I have NTSD," he said. "You ever heard of that? I think it means I'm just plain crazy."

"Yeah, I've heard of it. And it's P...TSD," I said.

"What does it stand for?" he asked.

"Post-Traumatic Stress Disorder," I said.

My sisters and I had talked on and off about what Dad was going through. My sister Kathleen had offered to send Dad a packet that included lots of information, treatment options, and other resources in it. I hadn't known she'd sent it, but I was glad she had.

The burden of carrying this had become heavy. Little by little, my life, my family, was showing the stress associated with trying to help someone through a traumatic experience. At times I was so tired and down and so overcome with grief for what my father had to live with that I felt alone. I didn't know a single person who had a father who was in WWII. I didn't know anyone who had a loved one who suffered from post-traumatic stress.

Now that I knew my sister had sent the PTSD information, I was relieved and scared at the same time. I didn't know if he was ready to face his problems in that way. And I knew that I would be the one to pick up the pieces if it backfired.

"What does that mean, post-traumatic...whatever?" Dad asked.

"Well, the way I understand it, it's not anything new. Other wars just had different names for it, like shell shock," I said. "I've looked it up on the Internet and they used to believe that it was caused by the loud sounds of the cannons or guns going off. But now they know that's not the case."

"Sometimes I just blank out," he said. "It's like everyone around me is going about their business but I'm back there. I'm with Mal on that ship. Do you think that's PTSD?"

"Probably," I said.

It was such an important moment and I didn't want to say something wrong. Now was my chance to help my dad. Maybe after all this time, I could finally point him in the right direction—one that had a chance of bringing healing to his soul.

"You know, Dad, we have the veteran's hospital right here in Walla Walla. I know they have counselors you can talk with."

"Oh, that's what your sister said. I got by all these years just fine. I'm not going to a shrink now. Shrinks are for crazy people."

He'd said that all my life. He didn't believe in psychiatrists, or psychologists, or even counselors. He'd often said that if you go to one you'll come out crazy for sure. I searched for just the right words. This was too important to mess up.

"Sometimes it just helps to talk to someone who understands, Dad. Counselors who work with veterans are different from regular psychiatrists. They understand the special things that go along with wartime problems. It just might help you to talk to someone," I said.

"I *am* talking to someone," he replied. "You."

I wanted to argue. I wanted to remind him that I didn't know what in the world I was doing. I wanted to tell him that this load was too heavy for one person and I was afraid I'd drop it somehow and he would be hurt. But I just smiled back.

"I don't even know how I went to the bathroom," he said. "On the plane and then in the hospital…I don't remember how I went to the bathroom. I mean, did I wet myself or did I use a toilet? I don't remember. It just drives me crazy, all this."

April 24, 1945

Dear Folks,

Back from liberty and three letters awaiting me—none in today's mail tho. According to my calculations my package should be here tomorrow. But I won't "eat my food before it comes."

Just an odd thought to make you jealous. At ships service we can buy all the pineapple juice we want for a dime a large can. It's ice cold and no [ration] points either. A few months ago it was a luxury but I've had so much of it—I'd just as soon drink good cold water.

Spent rest of the time working from one U.S.O. to another. Saw a couple shows. Ate hamburgers and ice cream all day. Sure glad you sent Andy Keve's picture—think I may be able to locate him thru the Red Cross. I saw his name on a U.S.O. register but just figured he was somewhere else like the rest of them. I still haven't seen a soul I know in civilian life.

Found out I can take my exam for a ranking anytime before the 15th of May and be rated June first. If the head officer wasn't so stubborn I wouldn't even have to take the exam. The rules concerning it state that a class "A" school graduate only needs a recommendation from his superior officer for a rate. But he claims I should know the stuff OK if I was so good in school so I'd just as well take the exam—boloney—anyway I'm studying again.

A paper boy told me he made close to ten bucks for a six hour day—seems a private enterprise is a better money maker than salaries. A person could start up anything and make money at it. All kinds of trailers made into hamburger stands with a steady stream of customers.

Guess I've never seen a stateside paper since I've been here. I'm kind of getting wise to the local ones. They put every shot fired into headlines. Maybe that's part of the propaganda campaign to make us more conscious—as if we could be any other way in this atmosphere.

Everyone seems to remember I'll soon be a year older. Been getting cards from all over. After all the rumpus, I'll probably spend the day as usual—on the job. I may celebrate by buying everyone a cigar for my birthday. Should be the other way around but what good would it do me, since I don't smoke. I just can't help smiling at everyone that has to stand in line for their ration of cigarettes, liquor and other unessentials. I sure save a lot of time.

Don't take Joe's prophesies to heart. I'm afraid I'll be here for a long time. Most of the boys around here have been here for 18 months and up so I can't expect anything better. I just figure on coming back when the Japs are licked which probably won't be too long now.

Some of the pessimistic ones say, "Golden State in '48—Bread line in '49"—mostly cause it rhymes well I think. But I expect to be telling all of you all about it long before that. Some one even predicting home for Christmas, but that's a little too pervious I'm afraid.

Couldn't locate any Fiat parts, but have two addresses to check with to find out when the owners get these parts. I'll do it. Next liberty, but don't get your hopes too high from Hawaii way.

Well g'bye for now. Write. Love, Murray

Since we'd started this journey, Dad had an interesting reaction to his letters. He was completely uninterested. He treated them like they were infected with the bubonic plague. He wouldn't touch them unless he had to. And the only time he had to was when we got together so he could help me decipher his writing. We were halfway through a bunch of letters when we kept getting confused on where we were in them. I'd turn to the wrong page, or he'd get the wrong paragraph. Frustrated, he decided to read the whole thing aloud. As he did, I went about the task of typing in any words I hadn't known. But then he got to the following paragraph:

Guess I've never seen a stateside paper since I've been here. I'm kind of getting wise to the local ones. They put every shot fired into headlines. Maybe that's part of the propaganda campaign to make us more conscious—as if we could be any other way in this atmosphere.

"Hmm…" he said.

He read it aloud again.

"What?" I asked.

"I think I was hinting at something here," he said. "That line about the propaganda campaign to make us more conscious. That was a hint at what I'd just been through. I knew that nobody had any idea what had really happened at Okinawa—the code-breaking part. The part about being overly conscious of the war—I was talking about being part of the top-secret team and being afraid to speak a word of it to anyone."

He sat quietly for a bit.

"So you did write about it," I said. "Well, sort of."

"Looks like I did," he said. "And it got past the censors too. They wouldn't have had a clue about what I was talking about anyway though."

I looked at him curiously. For a rare moment in our times together going over the letters, he looked pleased.

CHAPTER TWENTY-FOUR

Office Work

GLAD YOU SENT DADS LETTER ON, MOM. IT WAS VERY INTERESTING. HE REALLY HIT IT SWELL FOR THE FIRST PART OF THE TRIP....JUST HOPE THE REST OF IT WAS AS GOOD, BUT I HAVE MY DOUBTS.

I'M SURE ANXIOUS FOR NEWS ABOUT THE FIAT. IT SHOULD BE ROARING AROUND BY.NOW. COME TO THINK OF IT....ROARING IS THE WORD...I BELIEVE I BUSTED THE FLEXIBLE EXHAUST PIPE FOR YOU. DON'T FORGET, IF SOME OF YOU SHOULD GO AWAY TO COLLEGE SOMEWHERE AND MAYBE THE REST OF YOU WOULDN'T WANT TO BE SEEN IN A LITTLE FLIVVER LIKE THAT....I'D BE GLAD TO TAKE IT OFF YOUR HANDS....WITH MY FOUR BUCKS.....

WELL....I'D BETTER CLOSE....I'LL TRY NOT TO WAIT SO LONG NEXT TIME IN WRITING. WHAT WITH GOING ON LIBERTY....MY NEWS JOB AND BUILDING RADIO I SEEMED TO GET BEHIND AGAIN.

MURRAY W. FISHER S 1/C (RM) WRITE Love, Murray

Guys going by the hut all day, and now and then I hear someone say, yeah, listen to him copy that stuff... Only guy on the base that can copy it and he's only a seaman. That's the Navy for yuh—Ad infinitum—lots of fun.

—August 13, 1945

"Good news!" I hollered as I burst through Dad's front door.

Dad was in his usual place in the living room. I sat across from him, plopping my purse down on the floor and the notebook on my lap. I opened the notebook and then did my best Vanna White impression, sweeping the valuable merchandise with one hand.

"You know what this is?" I asked. "*This* is a typewritten letter!"

I had finally reached the letter dated April 29, 1945, and was ready to celebrate. After months of deciphering my father's tiny handwriting, I had made it to the first of the typed letters.

"Well," he said. "Now you won't need me at all. It'll be smooth sailing from here on out."

I got up and put the notebook on his lap.

"*Well,*" I said, "I wouldn't say that I won't need you now. I'll just be able to read the letters without needing you to decipher the words for me. But I still need you to decipher their meaning."

"Meaning, huh?" he said suspiciously. "I didn't sign up for that. What're you going to do with all this anyway?"

"Well, it started out with me just transcribing the letters so I could give a copy to each of the kids. But now, I want to tell the *whole* story, like fill in the blanks where the letters leave off."

"So you're adding more details," my father said.

"Yeah, something like that," I replied.

"What do you want me to do with this?" He lifted the notebook slightly.

"Read it," I said.

"Oh, I'm not going to do any such thing. Who cares anyway? It's just a bunch of letters," he said.

"But now they're easy to read. Thank God for the invention of the typewriter," I joked.

"Well, just because I *can* read them doesn't mean I *want* to," he said.

He closed the notebook and held it out.

I took it from his hands, a bit bewildered. I thought he would have enjoyed reading his letters at that point. Even though he seemed to have an aversion to them, I thought that maybe if the reading was easier, he'd be compelled to read them. He was a compulsive reader, after all. But he would have none of it.

"So, it looks like you somehow got to a typewriter. How did you manage that?" I asked.

He sat back in his chair.

"When they released me from the hospital," he began, "I started my office job. I think I actually got the job before I went to Okinawa, but I'm not sure."

He was relaxed. These memories came easily to him. There was no struggle or hesitation. I put the notebook in my backpack and sat back too.

"They put me in a place called Flag Detachment. That's where all the top brass were. I remember I kept being amazed when I'd see someone like Admiral Nimitz just walking down the hall. I tried to pretend that it was no big deal, but it was. I suppose it was an honor to be trusted to work there, but I figured even the top brass needed peons like me to type their letters and sweep their floors. Most of the time, those bigwigs weren't in the office at all anyway. It was in Naval Intelligence but there wasn't much to do with that once I returned from Okinawa."

"Did anyone talk to you about Okinawa? I mean, once you got the office job?" I asked.

"No," he said. "I always wondered if everyone knew or not. I thought maybe they were watching me to see if I'd lose it or something."

"So what was your job there?" I asked. "What did you do on a daily basis?"

He laughed.

"Well, for one thing, I had lots of spare time to write letters. Everyone I worked with did that. I was in a small office. The commander was right across the desk from me. He had a yeoman, which is like a secretary, who he dictated letters to all day. Well, one day the yeoman was sick so he had to settle for me. And for some reason I was able to dictate as fast as he could speak. So when the Yeoman returned, he fired him and kept me."

"What else did you do, besides take dictation from the commander?" I asked.

"Oh, I don't know. Nothing really," he said. "The war was really winding down."

He was right about that. His next letter, dated May 7, was V-E Day (Victory in Europe). Although he had yet to see an effect on the war in the Pacific, he was aware of what was going on elsewhere in the war.

May 7, 1945

Dear Folks,

No wise cracks about our railroad club, Mom. Everyone I told about it, suggested we line up some chairs around the room and play train.

The bank statement arrived and I just can't figure where all my thousands disappeared to. My treasurer made some poor investments no doubt. Oh well, easy come easy go.

Speaking of do-re-me, I have a total sum of 53 bucks now. I got paid as per usual a couple of days ago and added the sum to the pocketbook balance. Then a wild day of spending on liberty yesterday and I ended up with the aforementioned amount. Pretty good for a mere seaman. Don't tell anyone but maybe I'll save up enough to get the flivver painted by the time the war is over.

And speaking of war over—this is a momentous day I suppose. No one seems very excited over here tho. The European situation seems so remote from ours that it's just another battle to us. The war over here is big as life and looks very promising to last on for quite a while yet. No one seems to be celebrating at all and no one even mentions it in conversation. FDR and Ernie Pyles death were the important news as far as we were concerned. It's sure swell to have that much of it over now tho. Maybe things will shape up faster over here from now on. I sure hope so. I'd like to spend Christmas at home.

It's funny about mentioning exactly where you are. People usually guess sooner or later and probably someone right across the bay from me can say all he wants about the place in his letters but the censors here have strict orders to cut out any mention of the place in letters here so out it comes. But anyway you guess exactly where I am so it doesn't matter much anyway.

Well, when I get a leave now, I can fly right in to Walla Walla. That will really be swell. That is if some general doesn't bump me off and make me hitch-hike.

Well I don't want to make too much of a good thing. I seem to be getting more letters nowadays than when I was writing three a day. Guess I'd better get busy and answer a few for a change before they suddenly stop altogether.

Write. Love, Murray

CHAPTER TWENTY-FIVE

Life or Death

Mom, if you want perfect foot comfort, take the hula gals' advice, just go barefoot.—May 9, 1945

With his story now out in the open, I thought our conversations would be easier. And they were in some ways. But there were still times when the answers eluded him and it seemed that the harder he tried to remember something, the more evasive the answers became. Sometimes it *never* came to him.

Sometimes he'd even answer a question from weeks or even months earlier without seeming to know he was doing it. That was the case with his job after Okinawa. It had been several weeks since we'd talked about the work he did after coming back from Okinawa.

Mr. Ed's remained our constant. We were mid-conversation, between bites of our Benedicts, when he suddenly blurted out, "You know the one thing I just hated about that job? My boss, the commander, made me do the dirty work," he said.

I was drawing a blank. I didn't know what he was referring to. But he continued and after a bit more information, I realized just what he was talking about.

"There was this metal drawer that sat on top of a file cabinet. Inside were 4 x 6 cards and each card had the name of a sailor who was in amphibious forces but not assigned to be out there fighting. And it was the commander's job to go to that file and pick a name. Whoever he chose would be sent out to the war. Well, the commander wouldn't do it."

My father looked down as if searching for the picture in his mind. Then, to my surprise, anger flashed in his eyes.

"He made *me* do it," he said. "I argued with him. It was *his* job to do that. But he didn't want the responsibility. After all, what we were doing was replacing some poor guy who'd been killed. It was like Russian roulette. Well, I didn't win that argument. He *made* me do it. So, I decided I just didn't want to know the name. Each card had the name, rank, and special training of a sailor in amphibious forces. I'd go to that file, close my eyes or look away, and take the first card. I didn't want to know who I was sending."

"I never thought about that," I said. "I guess someone had to make those decisions."

"Yeah, well, it shouldn't have been me," he said.

Dad had stopped eating. Everything about him was tense. He was nearly gritting his teeth.

"There was only one time that I looked at the names on those cards. But I had to do it."

Now I was curious. I stopped eating too. At this point, with all we'd gone through together, anger seemed an easy emotion to deal with. There wasn't any guessing or pretending. It was a relief to be able to actually see an emotion in my father.

"Who was it?" I asked.

"Well, it was somebody I knew," he said. "A guy named Thomas Coldwell. We went to radio school together and he was a Dayton boy, just like me. We were always giving each other a hard time. We kept in touch, and we were both radiomen, so we tried to beat each other to the next rate classification. He was a good friend. Do you know what a Dear John letter is?" he asked.

I nodded. "It's a letter that someone writes to end a relationship or a marriage," I said.

"Yes. Well, so many guys got those, it made me glad I didn't have a girlfriend, or a wife for that matter. Well, this guy, he'd come around fairly often and we'd talk about the life we left behind. He had gotten engaged right before he was drafted. Well, one day he got one of those Dear John letters. He was more upset than I'd ever seen a man be. He was all torn up about it."

My father shook his head, remembering.

"Well, he rushed into my office one day," he continued, "and he said he wanted to volunteer to be sent out in the next Beach Patrol Party, or B.P.T., as we called them. Beach Patrols were the first ones to go ashore during invasions. It was well-known that they had an 85 percent casualty rate. He knew the guys being sent out were returning in body bags. So he said the next time there was a draft out, he wanted to be in it."

"What did you do?" I asked.

I watched my father's expression change. So much time had passed, and yet his emotions were raw, as if the events had just happened. He'd lost his best friend Mal. And now he was faced with losing another one. I wondered, *How much can one person take?* I watched him as anger turned to resolve.

"I decided right then that if his name came up, I wasn't going to put his name in," he said. "It was the only time that I had to look at those cards. I looked just to be sure he didn't get sent. I knew he was upset and even suicidal. But I couldn't let him go."

"And did his name come up?" I asked.

"It did," he said. "But I didn't turn it in. I put it back in the file, probably at the back. I didn't want it to come up again, and it didn't. Not long after that, I got a letter from him and he was aboard a supply ship, so I knew he was safe—well, safer than he would have been on a Beach Party Team anyway."

He looked down and then said, "I've been thinking about it a lot lately. You know, some poor guy got sent out in his place, probably died. And all because of that little decision I made."

I sat silent. Even the heroic act my father had just described could be twisted around to seem like a terrible one. There wasn't a guidebook for this kind of conversation. There was no etiquette book for decisions made with the best of intentions that ultimately result in someone's death. I felt so useless; he needed someone else to talk to, a counselor or something.

"Have you thought any more about talking to someone at the VA?" I finally asked.

"A shrink?" he asked. "I'm not going to see a shrink. Shrinks are for crazy people."

He shook his head adamantly, and then pulled his plate closer, forking a bite of egg and swirling it around in the cheese sauce.

"Dad," I said. "That's not true. A psychiatrist helps people with lots of things. Just like a regular doctor does. And the ones at the VA work with veterans every day. I think it would help you to talk to someone."

"I am talking to someone," he said.

"But I'm not trained at this, Dad. I don't know anything," I said. "*I've* never been in a war."

He shook his head emphatically.

I wanted to say, *Well, what if I am the reason that your nightmares and flashbacks have become more frequent and more vivid?* But I said nothing. We were so far into this process and, although I did believe that talking about it might help him, I wanted to offer him more.

After all he'd been through, he deserved the best treatment available. Maybe there was some special treatment for PTSD that would help him. Maybe talking to someone who'd been in war, who could truly understand him, would be the answer. I was just an adult daughter, one who'd only seen war on television or read about it in books. I couldn't even begin to imagine all the emotions involved in it: the trauma, the horror, the guilt.

I'd heard that there were support groups at the VA for Vietnam veterans and Iraq veterans. I knew that they had to have some sort of common ground with my father. He'd never even talked to someone with PTSD. I imagined it would make him feel less alone, less crazy, if he heard someone with a story that paralleled his in some way. He wouldn't feel so alone. As much as I loved him, and as much as my mother prayed for him, we could never be more than outsiders trying to understand.

On the other hand, here was my father, sitting across from me, sharing things he hadn't told anyone. Maybe he was right. Maybe talking to me *was* enough. I guess it would have to be, because like it or not, I *was* all he had, all he'd accept. I just prayed it was enough.

"You know what?" he asked, interrupting my thoughts. "Thomas came home to marry and have kids and probably grandkids."

"Did he ever know what you did for him?" I asked.

"No," he said soberly. "He never knew."

"Well, you did a good thing, Dad." I said. "Regardless of how many ways you twist it around, when it comes right down to it, you saved his life. And that is a good thing."

He almost smiled.

"I suppose," he said.

May 9, 1945

Dear Folks,

I guess this is the way I start most of my letters. Nothing new since last night when I last wrote. Have finished all my tests including the final with the exception of the procedure test. Haven't got up enough nerve to tackle that yet.

Got a letter from Thomas Coldwell today signed with a "RM 3/C". So I lose a dinner party next time we meet stateside. I bet him I would beat him to a rate before we left Farragut. Guess he beat me by a month. The censor had cut a big chunk of his letter but according to the rest of it, he has seen a lot of water and several new islands a long ways farther west, but no fighting as yet. I'll have to get off an answer to him later tonight.

Just got back from taking an anti-tetanus booster shot that comes around every six months. Now my right arm is beginning to get a little sore. Good thing I don't play baseball. The team here has a game tonight and some of them can hardly raise an arm.

The mail to this address comes in three times a day direct from the states so we are always looking forward to the new mail. We go after it three times a day. Tonight is my turn again.

You know, I think I'll start a foto album of scenes of things I see on the island. I've seen practically everything of interest and they have a lot of nice cards to be bought in town. I could make up a nice small album and then send it to you to look over till I get back.

I got another issue of the Chronicle Dispatch *yesterday. The* Waitsburg Times *hasn't gotten started yet tho. Newspapers are sure the post office's headache. So darned many of them come thru with names torn off and the majority are such a small printing that you have to stop and slowly examine each one instead of just glancing at each one as is the usual case in processing letters. We always have piles of it stacked all around that is lost or no address or address faded out. But the boys sure are glad to get them, so I guess it's all worth it. And it doesn't matter how old they are. They are still hometown news.*

Mom, if you want perfect foot comfort, take the hula gals' advice, just go barefoot. When it starts to rain here even the business people just roll up their pants legs and take off their shoes and socks and wade down main street in their bare feet. It's sure crazy to see a man about 80 years old with a dark tan and white hair (if any) walking down the street barefooted in bathing trunks and a polo shirt with loud pictures all over it.

As for the fiat. I guess it's OK to paint the wheels but I sure wouldn't advise painting the body unless you absolutely have to. I know from experience that it never produces a job that you can wax with much success. To give it a spray "factory" paint job at an auto shop later is almost impossible with out sanding all of the old paint off down to the bare metal. Then of course white sidewalls always look nice with a dark car. Usually needs at least 3 or 4 coats of that special side wall paint tho. Not regular paint. The good part about that is that you can always repaint them black any time you want or wash them or repaint them white if necessary.

Well the guys are beginning to holler for mail. I'd better get after it.

Write. Love, Murray

As I read about Thomas Coldwell in Dad's letter, I thought about how my father must have felt. After secretly putting his card back in the file, which probably saved his life, getting a letter from him must have been a relief. When Mal was killed, he'd been helpless to do anything. But when he had a chance to save another friend's life, he'd resolved not to let it happen again. Knowing the story surrounding Thomas Coldwell, I smiled. The man had come home to find love and live a fruitful life. And he'd never known that, thanks to my father, he'd literally dodged a bullet.

CHAPTER TWENTY-SIX

A Blurred Line

Really had a turnout at the [V-J Day] parade, on the ground too, according to the papers. It was all quite an experience.—September 2, 1945

When I pulled up to my parents' house to pick Dad up for breakfast, he wasn't watching out the window for me. So I went inside. Mom said he was out back and would be back inside at any moment. I sat beside her on the sofa.

"He's not doing so well," she said.

"I know," I answered.

At times he was so sad, so disconnected, that it hurt to be with him. He even seemed to have aged, his posture bent and his walk a shuffle. But more striking than the physical changes were the emotional ones. Many days when I saw him, he barely spoke. Having a conversation with him was stunted and awkward.

Worse, my sweet father now often shot his anger at my mother, and for the smallest of reasons. He yelled at her, belittled her, and argued. Mom would just stand there, her mouth turned down, silent.

When either of my sisters came home for a visit, they stayed at my parents' house. Invariably, within a few hours of their visit, one sister or the other would call me.

"He's just so mean," my sister would say. "Something's

changed. He just yells at her for nothing at all. Is he always like this now?"

I wasn't sure. Living just a few blocks away, I didn't have a reason to spend the night, let alone three or four days at their house. But on occasion, I would see the rage. It would be over something so simple. And my sisters told me the worst of it: he called my mother stupid.

And yet my mom, she simply took it. I don't know how she did it, but she did. It wasn't that she was made of stone and not hurt by his outbursts. But she knew on some deep level that perhaps only fifty plus years of marriage could explain: that something was wrong with him. It didn't make his words any less hurtful. But every time he hurt her, she prayed. And when he came back to hurt her again, she prayed even harder.

"He's having nightmares," Mom said. "Terrible nightmares, and he had a flashback the other night."

"What do you mean? What kind of a flashback? How do you know it was a flashback?" I asked.

"You know, when I thought about it later, I half remembered hearing running water in the middle of the night. But I didn't think anything of it. But when I went into the bathroom in the morning, there was water all over the sink and floor," she said. "I took some towels from the cupboard to clean it up and yelled for your dad."

My father had just stood there in the doorway as she soaked the water up.

"What in the world happened in here?" she asked.

"I had a flashback," he said. "It was like I was back on that ship with Mal. I think I was half awake and half sleeping. My mind just ran the whole thing like a video, but I was in it. I looked down and I saw his blood on my shirt. I was standing here washing it off when I sort of came to."

We heard the back door open. Dad walked into the living room, grabbing his coat and cane from the chair.

"How long have you been waiting for me?" he asked.

"Oh, not long," I said. "Just long enough to talk about you."

"That's what I'm afraid of," he joked.

He looked at my mother and then at me. Although he didn't let on that he suspected what we'd been talking about, there was something in his expression that looked suspicious. Still, neither of us spoke of it.

"Are you going to the Veterans Day parade?" he asked on the way to the restaurant.

"Maybe," I said. "When is it?"

"It's on Sunday," he said. "At ten o'clock."

"But that's right in the middle of church," I said. "Why would they have it on a Sunday?"

"That's just where it fell this year," he said.

I hadn't been to the parade in years. It just fell at a bad time. That's what I told myself. I enjoyed the Fair parade in early September, when the weather was still warm. There was a nighttime Christmas parade in December that was fairly new to our town. However, three parades in four months just seemed a little much.

But after the intense and emotional journey we'd been on, how could I not go with my father?

It was bitter cold that Sunday. Ric filled a thermos with hot cocoa and I put some cups in a plastic grocery sack. But when it came to taking the kids, they did not want to go. The most vocal was our youngest, Caleb.

"Do they throw candy?" he asked.

"No," I said. "That's the fair parade. November is just too wet and rainy for candy to be thrown on the street."

"Then I'm not going," he said.

"Caleb," I scolded. "It's not about the candy."

"Yes, it is," he argued.

"Listen, Caleb," I said. "Veterans Day is the most important holiday of the year. It's the day we honor people who fought to keep our country free. Think of all the things you can do, all the freedom you have. All of that is because veterans fought for it. Like your grandpa."

"Grandpa was in a war?" Caleb asked.

"Yes," I answered. "He was in World War II."

"Did he carry a gun?" he asked.

"I don't know," I said. "You know all those letters I've been typing up—of Grandpa's?"

"Yeah," he answered.

"Well, your grandpa did some really important things during the war. He broke a code called Katakana. And just like all of the young men who went off to fight, your grandpa was very brave. His country needed him and he went," I explained.

"You know other veterans too, like your uncle Rudy. He is a Vietnam veteran," I added. "And when people are in a war, they are never the same again. They come home to live their life, but they can never forget the things they had to do and the things they saw."

"And that's what the parade is for?" Caleb asked.

I nodded. Caleb, satisfied with my explanation, quickly put on his coat, hat, and gloves. Micah and Danielle had heard the conversation. They'd probably secretly hoped that Caleb would win this one, but he hadn't and they too dressed warmly.

We met Mom and Dad at the designated spot, arriving early so we'd get a good one. Dad had already set up folding chairs for him and Mom. They were bundled up and had wool blankets across their laps.

Ric handed me the thermos as he unfolded chairs for us. A sparse crowd gathered at the curb.

As the color guard passed, my father raised himself, with some difficulty, from his lawn chair. He removed his hat and held it over his heart.

I leaned down to whisper in Caleb's ear.

"Caleb, remember, we stand out of respect for the American flag and what it stands for," I said.

"But nobody else is standing," he whined.

I looked around, and then pointed out the few who were standing. After the flags passed, Ric served hot cocoa as we watched the parade. There were horses, vintage cars, and a few groups that marched by. Unlike the Southeastern Washington Fair parade or the Christmas parade, this one was sparse both in participants and in spectators. For a small town that was full of patriotic folks, this was a pathetic showing.

A short time later, the last of the parade passed us and we gathered up our things. Caleb looked up at me.

"That was it?" he asked.

I held his hand as we crossed the street.

"I thought you said this was *important*," he said.

I again told Caleb the importance of veterans and the freedom they've given us, but I knew it was a moot point. You can't fool a child; he'd already seen what people thought of Veterans Day. I couldn't change that.

May 31, 1945

Dear Folks,

It has been about three days since I wrote last. I suppose you think I'm at least at Guam by now. Surprise! I'm still here.

I wouldn't think a little thing like a ride home from Pasco would be much to worry about. Personally I would be glad to be turned loose over here in the middle of a pineapple field with orders to find my way back to Dayton.

I didn't beat you far as to seeing "Here Come the Waves." Saw it about a month ago. I notice most of the shows advertised in the Chronicle Dispatch *are about the same ones we have here at the same time. Don't tell anyone but I seem to know more about the DF news than Waitsburg news. That is except when they tell a bit about some old school chums. Saw Merle Eaton's picture in the* Times *for example. Sure hope he was just a prisoner in Germany and is OK now.*

I've often speculated too, as to what I'll do when I get back. I change my mind about once a week. I understand I can start school any time within two years after I'm discharged from the Navy under the GI bill of rights. I imagine at least another year in the service and then I'll be 25. That's darned near too old to start a regular college course of four years so imagine if I go to school at all it will be to Kinmans or some kind of business course of a year duration or a little more. Kind of hate to lose out on a chance to get some free higher education but on the other hand, I'll probably just lose out that much more time in getting caught up again on things on the railroad. I've thought quite a lot lately, that it might be a better idea to take a few weeks off (if I can stand it) when I get out and then work for a year or so on the railroad (at Helix I s'pose) and then take in a year of school. But you are probably right mom as to cash. I think I'll just run around until the dough runs out. That shouldn't be long, as I figure it will take most of the total three hundred bucks mustering out pay to get new clothes. But then, we have a few days yet. Another thing—men (good men) must be scarce. All my old gal friends are pitching in and really writing nice letters. They'll probably all be lined up at the depot and make me take my choice when I get back.

We got word a couple of days ago that the first four rows of tents along a main road here would have to be vacated in one hour. They assigned us to new tents about the same distance from the office—about 50 yards. I really hit it lucky there. I was put in a tent with four of the guys that practically run the school here. Of course I knew them all before but not too well personally. Two of them are storekeepers (Navy rate) who washed out of flight training last year. The other two are a radioman and signalman who are in the big shots.

We have the best tent on the base I think. They have a special floor of heavy painted plywood—smooth as glass and easy to clean. That makes it much cooler during the day. And the table in the center is varnished wood same as the individual chairs. We also each have a chest to put things in instead of living out of sea bag as before. Also have four radios now including mine. No use doing anything about sending it back tho as you never can tell about the Navy. I might be by myself again tomorrow. And the best thing about the change is the food. They all know all the cooks and bakers and do them favors now and then so we are well furnished all the time with any kind of meat anytime we want it. One of the men is a good cook so he does the cooking. Another takes care of the dishes and silverware. I drew keeping the table and floor clean. It's really a pleasure after living in that other tent. Had the best steak sandwiches tonite I've eaten since I hit the "rock." We really have a swell bunch. We all work together here and when it comes to any special favors now and then we can always help each other. I'm in the post office and of course can slip mail out a couple of hours or more early instead of waiting 'til mail call, and they can do me favors. That's the way the Navy is run so I just as well take advantage of it.

And mom whatdaya mean, me find socks for Iris. I'd be embarrassed to pieces buying stockings for a gal. And besides I'll bet they either don't have them or wouldn't let me send them anyway. I'll take off one day (real soon too) and see if I can find her some costume joolry. That's about all they have on the island.

Love, Murray

After the parade, as the kids went back to their lives, I looked around our house. Ric had made a fire in the fireplace. We had warmth. Homemade soup was warming up on the stove. The house was homey and comfortable. These were all things that my father didn't have during the war. He made the best of it, but it wasn't easy. In some letters he was so homesick, you could feel it. And in others, optimism dripped from the pages. More often than not, he was simply trying to make the best of a bad situation. He was thankful for the floor in his tent and the radio he listened to. *Try as we may,* I thought, *we can never really know what it feels like to be in a war, leaving home with just a few things; leaving absolutely everything that brings us comfort and joy. We can never really know what it means to completely lose control over even the most rudimentary of things.*

The next Wednesday, I felt like I had to say something. The showing at the parade of both spectators and participants was so poor that it had really upset me; I couldn't stop thinking about it. I was angry that in a small and patriotic town, it seemed nobody would take the time to simply participate in some way to honor our hometown veterans. I felt guilty that I too had ignored this simple ritual for so many years. I didn't know if Dad had thought about the parade or even cared. If he did, he hadn't let on. Still, I had to say something.

"I want to apologize," I said, as soon as he got in the car. "For the parade. I can't believe how few people were there. We owe the veterans of this town so much more."

Dad sat quiet in thought. "What I missed," he finally said, "was the marching band."

What a simple thing, I thought. He wanted just one thing; a marching band.

CHAPTER TWENTY-SEVEN

Write Your Mother

You know, I think I'll start a foto album of scenes of things I see on the island. I've seen practically everything of interest and they have a lot of nice cards to be bought in town. I could make up a nice small album and then send it to you to look over till I get back.—May 9, 1945

Some names in my father's letters were simply a mention, others were fairly regular. But one, Chad Broughton, appeared suddenly and then continued for several letters. From what I could ascertain, he was from my father's hometown but at some point was stationed on Oahu, just as my father was. My interest was piqued. Also, I tried my best to balance difficult questions with lots of informational and hence non-emotional ones. So it seemed like a good question to try.

It was a warm, late fall day, when I walked over to my parents' house. Dad was in the garage. He'd built a remote-controlled lift/carrier for his Segway on the back of his car and he was still fine-tuning it.

"Hi, Dad," I said.

"Well, hello there," he said. "How are you?"

"I'm fine. How are you?"

"I'm fine too," he replied. "I'm just trying to fix this thing so this part that holds the handlebars in place won't scratch my Segway when the car is moving."

He went on to explain and demonstrate it.

"Do you have time to sit for a bit?" he asked.

"Sure," I said. "I have something to ask you anyway."

He pulled a second lawn chair beside his on the grass, next to the flagpole. The leaves on the dogwood trees had just started to fall, laying a purple-brown blanket on the green grass.

"So, a question?" he asked.

"Yeah. Who was Chad Broughton?" I asked.

"Is Chad Broughton in my letters?" he inquired.

I nodded.

"I suppose he would be," he said. "Chad and his family were pretty well-known in Dayton. They were wheat farmers. They lived pretty close to our house and our mothers were good friends. Well, my mother and Chad's mother would talk quite often. My mother must have pulled out my letters or something, just to show her. Well, his mother was only getting about two letters a year. I suppose she was envious of the prolific letters my mother got, because I got a letter from my mother that said for me to tell Chad to write his mother."

We laughed at the thought.

"So you told him?" I asked.

"Well, see he came through where I was, but it was a huge place. I probably wouldn't have seen him if I hadn't hunted him down. He was what we called a 'ninety-day wonder.' He was a college boy and so he was sent somewhere for ninety days so he could be an officer. Turns out that, just by chance, he was assigned to the amphibs and was in command of a ship. It was an LTC, a landing craft with a ramp at the front. His job was to take surplus stuff out to sea, lower the ramp in front, and dump it into the ocean."

"What kind of stuff?" I asked. "Like war stuff?"

"Yes," he said. "That and lots of other things. One was a load of perfectly good jeeps, another was a whole boat load of typewriters; they were practically brand new. I hated to see it but that was to keep from overloading the economy at home when the war was over."

"I suppose they're still down there," I said.

My father nodded.

"So, did you tell Chad to write his mother?" I asked.

"Well, I felt kinda silly telling a grown man to write his mother. But I told him anyway," he said. "But I don't think he ever listened to me."

"Maybe that's why you started talking about him in your letters," I said. "So his mother would get the message through *your* letters."

"Probably true," he said.

"Well, you do write great letters," I said.

"I do?" he asked.

"Sure you do! You're a great writer. You describe things so well," I said.

"I don't know about that," he said. "I was just bored and writing letters was about as close to home as you could get."

"Well, whatever it was, your letters must have brought comfort to both mothers," I said.

"I suppose so," he said.

June 11, 1945

Dear Folks,

Today about 8:30 a.m. I was strolling down towards the pier to catch a boat to go across the bay and saw LCT 451—Chad Broughton's boat. Had just about ten minutes before the boat was to leave for my mail run but dashed over to the side of the 451 and asked one of the boys if an ensign Broughton was aboard. He said he was in charge but not aboard at present. Then he glanced down the dock a little ways and saw him and pointed him out to me. So I caught up with him for just about five minutes all together. Then I had to rush to catch my boat. His was in dry docks having a new screw put on that they lost somewhere. Then when I got back around ten I took off for his ship again and went aboard and we gabbed for a while. Then I had to get back at noon to pick up more mail and he said if I could get back by one, they were going out for a short run and I could go for a ride with them. So I rushed around like mad and made it back OK.

We went a couple or three miles down the bay to where he was supposed to anchor. He showed me all over the ship and introduced me to most of the men aboard her. Showed him some of the Dayton pictures I had with me (brought 'em along on purpose) and we gabbed until 4 pm. Then I caught a small boat back to my base. He's going to drop around to my office whenever he comes over here for supplies so I guess we'll see each other now and then.

In case his folks should ask, he looks like a million and all the men I talked to privately think he's a regular guy. It's a bit touchy at times with a 21 year old ensign in command of a ship and men 38 years old under him. But all of them say he's swell and knows his stuff. He was the only officer aboard but the other day another ensign came on with him so now he can get in to town or at least ashore more often. But we both agreed that we'd much rather be in Dayton. Really enjoyed the last two days.

I'm making a collection of pictures taken around the island for souvenirs and sticking them in a nice album. When I get a few more different ones I'll send the album home and then gradually send others and let you stick 'em in.

Did anyone ever tell you how the Navy describes getting paid? Well, to make a long story short, "the eagle screams next week" which means we get paid.

I just got a bright idea about a piston for the Flivver. Write to the Yakima Cycle Company. They used to handle all models of American bantam autos and several other midgets besides foreign make cars and motorcycles. Anyway it's an idea. I used to hang around there quite often when I worked there.

Well I'd better knock off for now. Saw the show "Christmas in Connecticut" last night. Not bad...not good.

G'nite. And write.

Love, Murray

I came home from work and made a sandwich. I thought about the letters my grandmother had received during the war. One thing was certain: my father wasn't your typical letter writer. Writing them seemed to mean as much to him as it did to his folks.

Instead of my usual routine of taking out the next letter and transcribing it, I went to the bedroom and took all four notebooks off the shelf. I sat down and stacked them on my lap. They were heavy. I opened each notebook and thumbed through a few pages, not looking for anything in particular. It was at that moment that I grasped the enormity of the volume alone and what it must have meant to my grandmother. She died before I was born, so I didn't know what she was like. But being a mother myself, I understood.

She raised her little boy in a small farming town. He graduated from a high school class of less than fifty students. After graduating, he followed in his father's footsteps and worked for the railroad. Seeking independence, he worked and lived thirty miles away in the tiny town of Helix, Oregon.

When the war started, she must have been relieved that he worked for the railroad, since that would afford him deferments from being drafted. But after four deferments of six months each, he finally got his draft notice.

Sending her son away must have been devastating. Surely she'd seen other mothers go through it—some whose sons returned safe and sound and some whose didn't. So she probably did what I would do; she busied herself with household chores and even took a job with her husband at the railroad depot. Through it all, with her son more than two thousand miles away, they shared one thing in common: the letters. Each looked forward to the mail every day, my father at mail call and my grandmother at the mailbox outside her door.

I made a decision that day. I wanted to see my father's childhood home. I wanted to see the house that his letters had arrived at nearly every day. I wanted to stand on the property. I wanted to see it for myself.

So the next Wednesday, instead of going to Mr. Ed's for breakfast, I proposed a little trip. I got to his house a little early.

"You're early," he said. "I haven't even shaved yet."

He started to get up from his chair.

"Wait a minute," I said. "I came early for a reason. What would you think of having breakfast in Dayton this morning?"

"Dayton?" he asked. "Why Dayton?"

"I want to see your childhood home, the one that you sent the letters to during the war," I said.

"Why?" he asked. "I'm sure there's not much there anymore."

"Well, I've got all your letters, but I want to see where they went to first—my grandmother's house."

He shrugged.

"There aren't any good breakfast places in Dayton," he said.

"What about that little A-frame place?" I asked.

"Yeah, I suppose we could try there," he relented.

"So, you're up for it?" I asked.

"Sure," he said. "I don't know what you expect to see. I don't even know if the house is there anymore."

"That's OK. I just want to see what's there."

We drove thirty miles to Dayton and found the A-framed diner that served breakfast. After eating, we drove to my father's childhood home.

My father knew the way by heart. He directed me, telling me to turn left here and right there. Just as I got comfortable knowing he'd let me know where the next turn was, he didn't. He apparently forgot I didn't know the way.

"Turn here. Turn here!" he said quickly.

"Well, ya gotta speak up a little sooner," I said, barely making the turn in time.

"Well, I *guess* so," he said.

We laughed together as he gripped the door handle when I rounded the corner.

It was a quiet street where it seemed like nobody was home. Huge, old trees framed the narrow road. I slowed down.

"Right here," he said. "It's that one…on the left."

I parked and grabbed my camera from the backseat.

"Do you want to get out?" I asked.

He shook his head.

I crossed the street. I was looking for one thing: the mailbox. Whether it was the same mailbox or not, I didn't know. But it looked old enough to be.

I looked up at the house. There was a small covered front porch framed by windows with the curtains pulled. I imagined my grandmother there, pulling the curtains back to watch for the mailman. Or maybe she stood on the porch, looking down the street for him.

My father got out of the car.

"What're you looking at?" he asked. He was unimpressed with this trip down memory lane.

"Everything," I said. "But mainly the mailbox. Just think, Dad, your letters…all of them…came right here to this house. All those letters that are in my bedroom right now came here first."

"Yeah," he said.

I took the camera from around my neck and snapped a few photos.

"Can I take a picture of you in front of it?" I asked.

"Why?" he asked.

"Because I want to," I teased.

"I guess," he said.

I snapped the photo. Something happened at that moment. It began in front of my grandmother's house but it grew over the next several days, until finally, I made a decision. I was going to tell the whole story. My father's story was about more than the letters he'd sent his folks. It may have begun with the letters, but the real story happened between them. And that's the story I intended to capture.

CHAPTER TWENTY-EIGHT

Anticipating the End

WAIPIO AMPHIBIOUS COMMUNICATION 15/Ct
TRAINING SCHOOL

7/4/45

TO WHOM IT MAY CONCERN:

It is respectfully requested that the bearer of this card FISHER, M. W. S1C be permitted to embark at landing "C" as he is on official business as mail carrier from the school.

W. P. Quinn, Lt., OinC

Over here of course, they had such a mess checking and rechecking my eyes that maybe someone decided I should be reclassified. Most special assignments are in that class due to bad eyesight or other minor ailments.
—July 6, 1945

I had bookmarked an Internet site with a WWII timeline of the war; every few days, before I would transcribe his letters, I checked the site to see what was going on in the world at that time. All over the world it seemed the war was coming to an end. But while the United States planned the invasion of Japan's mainland, Japanese Premier Suzuki announced that they would fight to the end rather than accept a conditional surrender. My father's letters reflected signs of what was to come.

July 6, 1945

Dear Folks,

Boy things sure look good for a direct invasion of Japan mainland any hour now. Everything will probably bust loose all at once pretty quick.

Heard some official scuttlebutt today that sounds swell for me. One of the officers told me so it's probably right although you never can tell when even one of them is stringing you along. They were talking about who they could ship out of here and who they were planning on keeping. One guy said they could ship almost everyone in the office out except for the ones who had over 18 months overseas and Fisher. Then someone asked how come Fisher and they said he's a "special assignment" man and can't be given any sea duty—he'll probably be the last man to close the doors of the old school when the rest of us leave. Doesn't hurt my feelings a bit. But I have no idea how I ever got to be Special Assignment.

I have no doubt but what I should have been from the start on account of the blinkers but I never was classified S.A. in the states. Over here of course, they had such a mess checking and rechecking my eyes that maybe someone decided I should be reclassified. Most special assignments are in that class due to bad eyesight or other minor ailments but can still do most any kind of routine behind the lines.

You know a few days ago I got a big thick soft new mattress almost like civilian days (except still no springs) and put it under my regular one and a half-incher. Boy I never had such a rough night since I hit the rock. Couldn't sleep at all. Thought I'd try it one more night and if no better sleeping, I was going to give it away. Guess I got used to "soft living" pretty easy cause in about 4 or 5 nights it was feeling pretty good for a change. Never realized what a difference it was (just another innovation we staff members have lately).

Well, I'd better get a letter off to someone else for a change. Write soon.

Love, Murray

It was another late night when I read his letter. Everyone was in bed. Only the ticking of my grandmother's clock could be heard. Cocoa curled up next to me, her warm body pressed against my leg. I read the letter as I transcribed it. But when I was done, I read it again. This letter was a turning point. Something was finally happening. After all the mundane daily duties he'd endured since coming back from Okinawa, the cadence of his words picked up. He was hoping beyond hope that it would be over soon.

But as everyone around him prepared to leave for the invasion of Japan's mainland, my father learned that he would not be among them, and he didn't know why. How could he not have known? It made sense to me; he'd had a breakdown that had landed him in a military hospital just two months prior. My best guess was that by classifying him as Special Assignment, they were keeping him close in case he had another breakdown. As the nurse had said several weeks prior, he was fine physically, but on that ship off of Okinawa, he'd lost a piece of time. A part of his mind, his memory, was gone. Or perhaps Special Assignment was a way to assure that the investment of time they had put into my father teaching him Katakana would be carefully protected.

But what struck me the most about that paragraph was the line, *I have no idea how I ever got to be Special Assignment*. Just a few short months after the trauma of losing his friend, my father did not know what was special about him. He'd already begun the process of wrapping the memories up so tightly that they would remain so for more than fifty years.

Was that good or bad? I couldn't be sure. On one hand, he was able to easily transition back to his pre-war life. But on the other hand, those memories came back with a vengeance later. Maybe it would have been best dealt with early, when he was still in his twenties. But that time passed and all we could do now was deal with it as best we could.

CHAPTER TWENTY-NINE

The Bomb

Signed at TOKYO BAY, JAPAN at 0904 I
on the SECOND day of SEPTEMBER, 1945

By Command and in behalf of the Emperor of Japan
and the Japanese Government

By Command and in behalf of the Japanese
Imperial General Headquarters

Accepted at TOKYO BAY, JAPAN at 0908 I
on the SECOND day of SEPTEMBER, 1945,
for the United States, Republic of China, United Kingdom and the
Union of Soviet Socialist Republics, and in the interests of the other
United Nations at war with Japan.

Supreme Commander for the Allied Powers

United States Representative

Republic of China Representative

United Kingdom Representative

Union of Soviet Socialist Republics
Representative

Commonwealth of Australia Representative

Dominion of Canada Representative

Provisional Government of the French
Republic Representative

Kingdom of the Netherlands Representative

Dominion of New Zealand Representative

Just heard the official answer to Japan's offer should come within forty-eight hours at the most. According to the latest press wireless release, they expect it any hour now.—August 10, 1945

My father's letters thus far were full of descriptive writing, so I expected the same even as the war was coming to an end. What I didn't expect was that he'd been right in the middle of events that would change the courses of hundreds of thousands of people. As I read on, I learned that he wasn't simply sitting on his bunk waiting for someone to announce the war's end; he was the one doing the announcing. It was another turn in his WWII life that he'd neglected to tell me.

When I discovered his part in it, I thought about how to best approach him. In my work with children, I'd learned that if you wanted to know more, it worked best to use open-ended questions, ones that can't be answered with a simple yes or no. So the next week, as we waited for our eggs Benedict to be served, I asked about what I'd read.

"What is press wireless?" I asked. "It's in your letters. Apparently, you were pretty good at it."

"I was, actually. I learned it at the same place I learned Katakana, at Farragut Naval Base. I was very fast at it. The news in those days would come in fast and furious, and it was important that they had someone who could listen to those dots and dashes coming in and get them typed out into plain English."

"So, it was Morse code, like dots and dashes?" I asked.

"Well, technically it was international code, but yes, dots and dashes," he said.

Everyone on the base, including my father, knew that after taking Okinawa, the next step would be to send our troops to mainland Japan. Mass casualties were expected. But then something that wasn't expected happened.

My father was relaxing in his bunk when an officer came rushing in and ordered him to go copy the press wireless that was coming in from Washington, DC. At first he thought it would just be a quick message. But the hours wore on with more and more information coming in. He and another man who could copy the high-speed code worked around the clock, having their meals brought in. They were two of just a few on the base who knew how to do it.

"I even got steak," he remembers. "And real butter. Real butter was a luxury in those days."

All across the base, word spread that something important was happening and that there was this guy who could copy press wireless at unbelievably high speeds. Soon, sailors and officers from all over the base came to see what was going on. My father would hear people walk by saying, "Yeah, that's the guy. His name is Murray Fisher and he can copy that stuff really fast."

But as hours turned into days and nights, he was getting tired. He was falling asleep at the typewriter. He was in dire need of some sleep. A bed was brought in for him, but once his head was on the pillow, he was afraid he would miss something important. He was only able to get a few hours of sleep here and there.

Then something strange came across the wire. It was called an atomic bomb.

August 9, 1945

Dear Folks,

I suppose you are thinking I could be anywhere in the world by now. But I just couldn't get started writing letters this week.

A lot of things have happened in the short (?) time I've been across—Iwo Jima, Okinawa, and V-E day and then of course the atomic bomb. And yesterday, Russia on our side and actually in the fighting already. Of course you've read as much about it all as I have so there's no use discussing it especially. Just think, V-J Day might even be on the day you receive this. It's just unbelievable. To think that eleven pounds of uranium bomb indirectly bring an end to such a terrible war. Of course everyone is jubilant over the possibility that it will be over in a matter of hours or maybe days or weeks, but no wild celebrating like you'd imagine.

Someone discovered I could copy the faster press and as it seems the faster the code comes over, the later the news is, I was elected as official press wireless man at the communication school and indirectly, the base. I happened to be copying some press from Guam on the morning of the first atomic bomb, for the officers to read. They foned the base officers and they ordered me to work out about six press schedules a day (and night if necessary). I copy the news and have a staff of four other men who rewrite it, edit it and make a few dozen mimeographed copies to distribute around the base for the men to read. I like it, but this is still the Navy. They just take it as a matter of course that a radioman should be able to copy fast press and that's all. My task was to copy incoming news [via international code]. I copied one schedule at about 23 WPM, three at about 35 WPM, one at about 40 WPM and one at 45 to 50 WPM [the more important the message, the faster it came across the wire]. The latter is really hot stuff and keeps me jumping to get it all. I usually get about three fourths of it and guess at the rest. Don't know just how soon it was after the news was sent over the press wireless about the atomic bomb, but it was a half hour before it was announced over the radio after I got it.

Remember me telling you a long time ago when I was in Farragut about copying a message saying B-29's had bombed Mt Fujiyama and it was erupting? That turned out to be what is called a dummy message and I thought for a while I had made a mistake and got on the wrong frequency and copied another of the same type...only the atomic bomb story seemed too fantastic to believe at all. One little bomb wiping out a city almost three times the size of Spokane. But it was true of course. News is changing so fast that I can't hardly keep up with it. Headlines changing hourly. One hour the new bomb. The next Russia declares war on Japan. Then another bomb on Nagasaki and this evening Russia has already advanced almost fifty miles into Manchuria. Then the best news of the war for us amphibs, is the announcement by our amphib admiral Turner that it was very possible that amphibious warfare would not be needed to take Japan. Of course that was just following what we had already guessed anyway. Well, anyway that's how it happened around here.

Another little thing—when I took it in to some of the boys, the first news cast I mean, they read it over and a couple handed it back and laughed and said, "Where'd you pick up that scuttle-butt Fisher?" The boys in the post office just laughed at me when I told them about one bomb destroying a few hundred thousand people. Of course they were half-way kidding, but got a lot of fun out of telling me I was getting rock-happy. You see, I've been copying press off and on and bring in a copy now and then to the office boys to see and in amongst a few paragraphs of news I make up a paragraph of my own...maybe about one of the boys being sent home or being awarded a medal or something. Just in fun...well, that's all that. It still seems almost impossible to believe.

Write. Love, Murray

The United States had dropped an atomic bomb, first on Hiroshima and then on Nagasaki. When the message was posted on a bulletin board nearby and copies began to circulate, Dad heard numerous men say, "What's an atomic bomb?"

"And then we started to hear that this atomic bomb had taken out a whole city," he said. "At first we thought that maybe this was just a dummy message, a fake one. Surely one bomb couldn't do all that. But as details came in, we realized it was true. Then someone turned on the PA system. We only used that for emergencies, so you knew if you heard anything broadcast over it, it was serious. Well, they read what I had copied and no one could believe it, so they started to come around in droves, asking if it was really true. Of course, I didn't answer any questions. I just kept copying the code."

Our breakfast had been served and was half eaten, and he

was still talking. Just when I'd thought that I knew all I could about his wartime experiences, he surprised me again. This time, instead of using the top-secret Katakana, he'd used the more common international code. Several times over the next few days, he was called upon to copy the code. Finally, there was reason to celebrate. He may have been too tired to join in, but his comrades weren't.

August 10, 1945

Dear Folks,

Well, looks like the big day is here. At least the big four are momentarily expected to come out with the acceptance of Japan's offer of peace. Finished writing you the three-pager last night at around midnite and decided to copy a little press to see how things were coming, so went over for about an hour, then went to bed at one. At three a.m. everything seemed to bust loose at once. Was in my tent about a block from the office. Someone came in and woke me up looking for the keys to the office and the radio was blaring Japan offers peace if we save Hirohito (or words to that effect). I hopped in my clothes and we opened up the office and turned on the P.A. system that is used to call men to the office in case of emergency, on and blasted out with the news. Lights started popping on all over and guys whooped and hollered for the rest of the night. I went right to work on my press sked and got an early copy. Now it's noon and haven't been out of my chair except to get a drink. With new news busting loose every few minutes it's pretty hard to leave things up in the air. The radio is almost as fast as the press wireless today.

By the way, do you remember a Betty Moat, a girl whose father used to live in Dayton but now in England? I wrote her when I had nothing better to do one day after reading of her in the C.D. and promptly forgot all about it. A while back, got an answer from her and it was written on V-E day in England. She described all the reactions of the different people and the celebrations everywhere. Think I'll write her on V-J day and do the same. Guess it's not officially here yet, but everyone is pretty happy just the same. Just heard the official answer to Japan's offer should come within forty-eight hours at the most. According to the latest press wireless release, they expect it any hour now. They also say leaving Hirohito on the throne won't make any difference. Have been hearing so many peoples opinions on the subject that I'm just getting tired and sleepy. About all I want to do now is sleep for a couple of days.

We had a bunch of LCI's (Landing Craft Infantry) left yesterday (about a hundred I believe for San Francisco, Seattle and Alaska and over to Russia for delivery there. Also another hundred were supposed to leave today. The latest reports cancelled both the crews orders.

It's like that Gal Miss Moat said, after so many years of war, it's hard to believe the fighting is all over and peace is here again.

'Twas a surprise to hear that the atomic bomb was made in Hanford too. Don't suppose any of them knew what it was they were manufacturing tho.

Personally, I'm not doing any celebrating myself, but will probably celebrate Sunday by going to church in Honolulu and guzzling a double chocolate milkshake.

That's all. Bye for now.

Love, Murray

We'd finished our breakfast and Biby had cleared our table. But neither of us was anxious to leave. I wanted to hear the rest of the story, and he wanted to share it.

"Sounds like everyone was pretty excited on the base after your press wireless copy was read," I said.

"Oh, they were," he said. "You could just hear a loud chorus of guys yelling and celebrating. It was really something. Of course, I had orders to keep copying the press wireless, so I had to concentrate on that. And I was so tired. All I really wanted was to sleep."

All over the base, rumors continued to fly, but the best one was the rumor of peace.

August 13, 1945

Dear Folks,

I'm so sleepy, I'll probably mess this letter all up, but thought I should write. Since the first atomic bomb hit and the Japs asked for surrender terms, I've been on whats called a continuous watch. That is a "press watch" that means that someone brings in my meals to me and I just drink lots of coffee and try to stay awake. That's what comes from being so indispensable. I have a cot in the room and lay down every few hours with earphones. Also have a couple of the instructors with me so when I drop off—which is often—they listen and when WCX New York comes on they wake me up and we take off again. Can't remember how many hours I've been on now but it seems like forever. I can type one station with one hand at 25 wpm and drink a cup of coffee at the same time. What a life.

They keep the place quiet and no one bothers me so it's not at all bad. I really enjoy it in a way, as it's something no one else can do. Guys going by the hut all day, and now and then I hear someone say, yeah, listen to him copy that stuff. He's the guy that's been going for several days now. Only guy on the base that can copy it and he's only a seaman. That's the Navy for yuh—Ad infinitum—lots of fun. With the peace rumor yesterday at 3:04 p.m. our time things really busted loose all over the island. They had a few recorded speeches made especially for the occasion and a parade in town. Everything went according per sked until a couple of minutes later it was announced a false report. Didn't bother me any as none of it came over the wire except a few minutes later when it told of both sides of the story. Everything on the island is really buzzing with rumors and I'm looking for a big celebration when it all ends for sure. Looking for it today sometime or possibly in the early morning. Then I'm going to sleep for about a week.

Have an order out now stating that only five percent of mail will be censored after V-J day. That won't mean much until it is cut out all together as it would still be impossible to say anything as your letter might be one of the five percent. I have a little something to tell you about stuff and things when they lift it all together.

Love, Murray

It was over. The war was finally over. The celebrating continued for several nights, but my father didn't take part in it. He slept through it all.

Reaching the end of the war in his letters left me with mixed emotions. The journey through them was nearly over. His secrets were brought to the surface. Yet, it still felt unfinished. I sensed there was another part to this journey. I just didn't know yet what it was.

CHAPTER THIRTY

Waiting

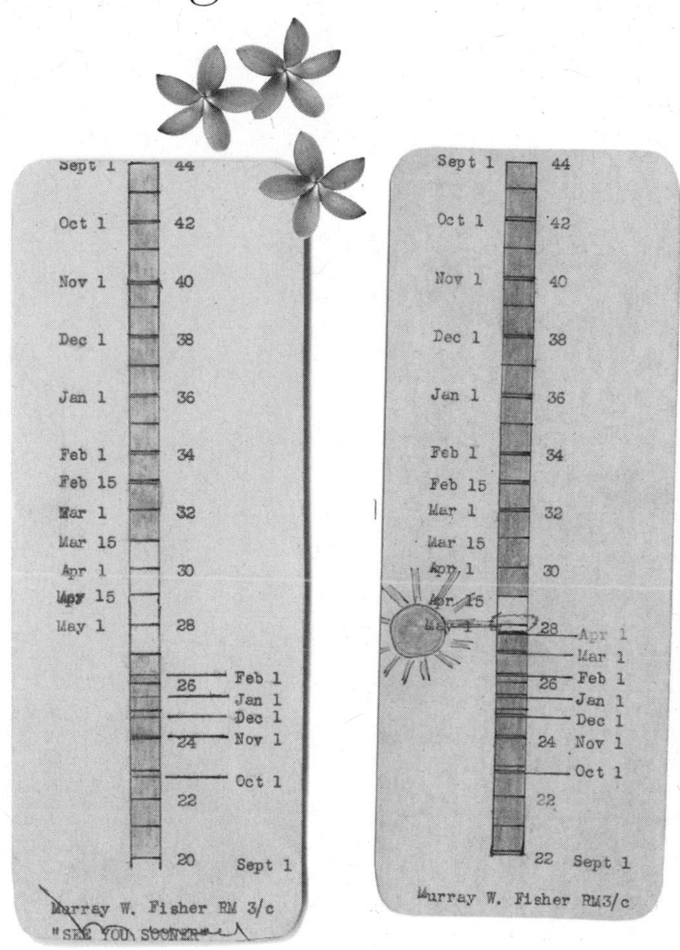

Now the Navy point system has come out, which finds me sadly lacking…They come to a miserable twenty out of the needed forty-four.—August 16, 1945

"The usual," my father said, as we sat down at our regular table at Mr. Ed's, before the waitress had a chance to ask.

"And extra sauce," she said.

My father smiled. It's a good feeling when someone knows what you want before you ask for it. But it's even nicer just to be known.

"So, I'm at a pretty exciting place in the letters," I said.

"Oh?" my father asked.

"Well, the war is over," I said. "That's pretty exciting, right? All that's left to do is send everyone home."

Dad laughed at my naiveté.

"What?" I asked.

"Well, that's not exactly how it works," he replied. "I guess I can try to explain it."

He took out his pen and slid his paper placemat to the middle of the table. He drew a thermometer, making marks on the side of it.

"You had to reach a certain number of points to get to go home. You got points for the missions you were sent on. You got a certain number for being overseas. I think they figured in if you were married or had kids. So in a sense you are right," he said. "Some of the guys did get to go home right away. But those were the ones who already had a lot of points."

"I never thought of it like that," I said.

"Everyone made those thermometers. Guys had them on their desk or in their lockers. I made a lot of them. I sent several home to my folks and then I'd tell them in my letters what number I was on," he explained.

August 16, 1945

Dear Folks,

Well, a lot has happened in the past two weeks. A month ago I thought I'd be coming home in about a year. Now it looks like two years. The place really went wild the evening after V-J day was declared official. You've probably read about it all from in the paper. I didn't do a thing except go to my tent and slept from about 7 p.m. until noon the next day. And I'm still sleepy. Back on the old schedule again.

Now the Navy point system has come out, which finds me sadly lacking. You've probably figured mine up. They come to a miserable twenty out of the needed forty-four. Of course most of the boys in the comm. school here are old timers who have been in a long time. Think I have about the lowest score in the staff. The next one to me is twenty-two. The majority seem to have around 30 to 40 and about six have the 44 and this morning they were filling out forms for discharges.

As for me, you have as good a guess as I have. Of course there aren't too many in the 44 point bracket so they are sure to lower the points right away. But it's a long long way to twenty points. No one has any idea what will happen to the rest of us now. Whether they are going to make a receiving station out of the school as rumored or just drop it like a hot spud like they are doing all other places. Then they could send us as a unit to the states or farther out. Your guess is as good as mine. Anyway don't kill the fatted calf just yet. According to Uncle Sam that duration plus six months doesn't start until the president or congress gets good and ready. In the last war I think someone said it was set at eight months after the armistice but congress didn't ratify it and it dragged on until 1921. That doesn't sound so hot. Personally it looks to me like everyone who wants to be a civilian again, will be out within a year anyway. But you never can tell.

What the guys are griping about most out here is the bill they are trying to get thru congress to stop the draft completely. That's just like a stab in the back to us. It doesn't seem very fair to stop drafting the men when we are still out here. If more new ones came in we would be going home and out much sooner. Well, that's about all of that.

We hear most of the rationing has been lifted in the states, including gas. That would have been more welcome news to me than the declaration of V-J Day. Here it doesn't mean a thing, to me. It's been stopped here too but who cares. You know another thing about the point system—I think it's about the fairest they could get. Of course the boys here with lots of battle stars and medals and months of hazardous overseas service really think it's terrible. Especially one guy whose been here just a little while but went thru Iwo and Oki and he has way less points than a boy who works in the post office and has his mother dependent on him, but he hasn't been out in a combat zone at all. Personally I've always thought, even if I'm overseas myself, that it isn't very fair to give extra credit for things like the above when the individual hadn't a thing to say about where he went or how much action he saw.

The base has changed around a lot. Everything at one end is being taken over by civilians, and the offices on the base and everything else is being moved down to one end. Just means I'm going to get even less exercise than before. Everything is within a couple of blocks of my tent now.

Oh almost forgot, as usual I'm late—this couldn't possibly get there in time, but a happy birthday to you mom. Have a birthday present for you and Ray both—not the same thing but just couldn't seem to get time to send it. I'll send it first class mail so will probably be there about the fifth of September.

Write. Love, Murray

P.S. Woe is me…I'll be glad when this is all over. They announced that all men with 44 points or more were on standby status and to lash their gear. What a lucky break—for them.

The war was over, but he didn't get to go home. I'm sure my grandmother was relieved. She knew her son had survived the war. If it were my son, I'd probably have been thinking of ways I could get to him. I bet my grandmother considered that too. But travel wasn't as easy as it is today and Hawaii was barely known at that time—known to most only as the place where Pearl Harbor was bombed. So once again, she turned to his letters as a source of comfort.

My father too must have been frustrated. I'm sure he would have agreed to any mode of transportation to anywhere just to get closer to home. It must have been bittersweet to see his comrades leave, happy for them and yet wondering when his day would come.

Dad and I had been through this journey together in a way. We'd started at boot camp. I'd watched as he dealt with tragedy and now the end was near. But this experience with his youngest daughter hadn't been the source of any kind of closure for him. He continued to have periods when he was agitated and angry, almost always aimed at my mother.

But there was something more than that. He was so down. Sometimes when I'd drop by to visit, he'd barely speak two words to me. Even when I asked about his newest project, he gave a minimal amount of information. There were times when he seemed upbeat, but they came less and less. There was no sparkle in his eyes.

In the telling of his secrets, he'd lost himself. He derived no peace from the experience. I'd hoped it would be cathartic. But it wasn't. He still remained as far away as ever.

CHAPTER THIRTY-ONE

Finding the Words

OAHU, T.H.
AUGUST
SEPTEMBER 2, 1945

DEAR FOLKS,

WELL, THIS SHOULD BE THE LETTER TO ENDALL LETTERS....ALL CENSORSHIP HAS BEEN LIFTED AS OF TODAY SO HERE GOES NOTHING....FIRST OF ALL THINGS HAPPEN FAST WHEN THEY GET STARTED IN THE NAVY, AS YOU ALREADY KNOW...YESTERDAY SOMEONE CALLED AND WANTED FIVE RADIOMEN TO ACT AS VOLUNTEERS TO BE IN THE V-J DAY PARADE TODAY IN HONOLULU. ONLY IT WASN'T EXACTLY IN THE PARADE...YOU SEE THEY WANTED TO PUT ON A DEMONSTRATION OF RADIO COMMUNICATIONS BETWEEN THE AIRPLANES AND GROUND AT THE REVEIWING STAND IN DOWN TOWN HONOLULU....ONE EACH OF US RADIOMEN HOPPED A FAST BOAT OVER TO FORD ISLAND A FEW STEPS FROM HERE AND GOT OUR RADIO GEAR ABOARD FIVE B-24'S AND TOOK OFF ON A FEW PRACTICE SESSIONS. THAT IN ITSELF IS SURPRISE ENOUGH I GUESS...THAT IS FOR US LAND GOING SAILORS BUT THEN......ANYTHING IS A SURPRISE. THEN XXXXXR TODAY WE GOT ABOARD AGAIN FOR THE FINAL TEST BEFORE THE PARADE AND EVERYTHING WENT OF PERFECT...THEY HAD LOUD SPEAKERS IN FRONT OF THE REVEIWING STAND AND ALSO BROADCAST PARTS OF OUR CONVERSATIONS OVER THE TWO LOCAL RADIO STATIONS....OF COURSE THEY HAD THE REGULAR RADIOMEN IN THE B-24 CREWS BUT THEY JUST HAVE REGULAR COMM. EQUIPMENT....OURS WAS PORTABLE....YOU WOULDN'T KNOW IT IF YOU HEARD IT BUT ITS THE MODEL "61Ø" WHICH IS A SMALL PORTABLE SET...ITS CALLED THE "WALKIE-TALKIE" BUT NOT AS SMALL AS WHAT THE PUBLIC CALLS THE WALKIE TALKIE...IT CAN BE CARRIED BY ONE MAN ON A PACK BOARD IN A PINCH BUT IS REALLY TWO MAN GEAR. THE LITTLE TINY TWO WAY HAND PHONE IS REALLY CALLED THE "HANDIE-TALKIE"...NOW YOU SHOULD BE MORE MIXED UP THAN EVER....ANYWAY THATS HOW IT WAS....AS MUCH A SURPRISE TO ME AS TO YOU....THERE WERE A FEW HUNDRED PLANES IN THE AIR ALL AT ONCE....AS FAR AS YOU COULD SEE IN EVERY DIRECTION WERE PLANES OVER EVERY TYPE....ARMY NAVY AND MARINE......FROM F7F'S TO LITTLE CUB OBSERVATION PLANES. REALLY HAD A TURNOUT AT THE PARADE ON THE GROUND TOO ACCORDING TO THE PAPERS. IT WAS ALL QUITE AN EXPERIENCE....

THEN FOR SOME MORE NEWS......WHICH WILL ALSO BE A SURPRISE...REMEMBER WHEN I FIRST LANDED ON THE ISLAND AND WAS UP FOR DRAFT A COUPLE OF TIMES AND GOT TAKEN OFF? WELL, I REALLY WASN'T TAKEN OFF THE DRAFT...ON ACCOUNT OF I COULD COPY THE JAP KATAKANA CODE THEY TRANSFERRED ME TO NAVAL INTELLIGENCE AND RIGHT AWAY I AND FOUR OFFICERS CAUGHT A PLANE FOR EAST POINTS...UP TO NOW OF COURSE COULDN'T BREATHE A WORD BUT GUESS ITS OK THIS TIME....AT THE TIME, WE HAD NO IDEA WHAT WAS UP, BUT WENT BY PB2Y I BELIEVE IT WAS...ANYWAY A FOUR MOTOR SEA-PLANE THRU THE JOHNSON ISLANDS AND ON DOWN TO GUAM AND THEN THRU TINIAN AND SAIPAN WHERE WE STOPPED FOR ALMOST A DAY....GETTING EQUIPMENT AND ORDERS. THEN WENT TO ANOTHER SMALL ISLAND ALONG THE XXXXXX THE ROUTE AND CAUGHT THE SUB "SAILFISH" WHICH YOU'VE PROBABLY READ ABOUT BY NOW...IT USED TO BE CALLED THE SQUALUS YOU KNOW AND WAS RECHRISTENED....ANYWAY THE WHOLE THING WAS PRACTICALLY A REPTTITION SCENE FOR SCENE OF THE SUB "COPPERFIN" IN THAT MOVIE "DESTINATION TOKYO"...ONLY WE WENT IN TOWARD "IWO JIMA". OF COURSE THEN, IT DIDN'T MEAN A THING AT ALL TO US....IT WAS SUPPOSED TO BE OCCUPIED BUT NO ONE HAD ANY INKLING AS TO HOW HEAVILY....THIS WAS ALL ON D DAY MINUS FOUR....OR FOUR DAYS BEFORE THE AMERICAN INVASION BY THE FIFTH MARINES....ALL FIVE OF US HUNTED UP THIS JAP FREQUENCY THAT WAS SENDING CODED MESSAGES AND COPIED IT (ALL WAS IN THE JAP KATAKANA) AND ONE OF THE OTHER OFFICERS WHO WAS A CRYPTOGRAPH SPECIALIST...GOT OUT HIS MACHINES AND TRIED TO BREAK IT DOWN...AND SUCCEEDED RIGHT AWAY....WE WORKED ON THE SUBS DECK ALL THE TIME IN PITCH BLACK NIGHT FOR ABOUT 18 HOURS....NEVER A PATROL PLANE OR SHIP CAME WITHIN SOUND OF OUR RADAR....

Then for some more news, which will also be a surprise. Remember when I first landed on the island and was up for draft a couple of times and got taken off? Well, I really wasn't taken off the draft.—September 2, 1945

In all of the time he had been at war, my father's letters were censored by the army. So I never expected to find any direct information about his code-breaking work in them. Even after the war ended, I assumed he'd leave that out of his letters.

"I was thrilled when they lifted all censorship," he'd told me. "But I still didn't tell my folks exactly what I'd done during the war. I told them part of it, but I didn't want my mom to worry, so I figured I'd just tell her when I got home. Plus, I knew there were still things I couldn't talk about. Whenever you work in intelligence, the military will let you know in writing when you are free to talk about your work. And I hadn't received anything in writing."

But then, I came to a letter that changed everything.

September 2, 1945

Dear Folks,

Well, this should be the letter to end all letters. All censorship has been lifted as of today so here goes nothing. First of all things happen fast when they get started in the Navy, as you already know. Yesterday someone called and wanted five radiomen to act as volunteers to be in the V-J Day parade today in Honolulu. Only it wasn't exactly in the parade—you see they wanted to put on a demonstration of radio communications between the airplanes and ground at the reviewing stand in down town Honolulu. One each of us radiomen hopped a fast boat over to Ford Island a few steps from here and got our radio gear aboard five B-24's and took off on a few practice sessions. That in itself is surprise enough I guess, that is for us land going sailors. But then…anything is a surprise. Then today we got aboard again for the final test before the parade and everything went off perfect. They had loud speakers in front of the reviewing stand and also broadcast parts of our conversations over the two local radio stations. Of course they had equipment. Ours was portable you wouldn't know it if you heard it but it's the model 610 which is a small portable set—it's called the "walkie talkie" but not as small as what the public calls the walkie talkie. It can be carried by one man on a pack board in a pinch but is really two man gear. The little tiny two way hand phone is really called the "handie-talkie." Now you should be more mixed up than ever. Anyway that shows it was as much a surprise to me as to you. There were a few hundred planes in the air all at once—as far as you could see in every direction were planes of every type—Army, Navy and Marine. Really had a turnout at the parade, on the ground too, according to the papers. It was all quite an experience.

Then for some more news, which will also be a surprise. Remember when I first landed on the island and was up for draft a couple of times and got taken off? Well, I really wasn't taken off the draft. On account of I could copy the Jap Katakana code, they transferred me to Naval Intelligence and right away I and a few others caught a plane for east points. Up to now of course couldn't breathe a word but guess it's OK this time. At the time, we had no idea what was up, but went by PB2Y I believe it was—anyway a four motor sea-plane thru the Johnson Islands and on down to Guam and then thru Tinian and Saipan where we stopped for almost a day—getting equipment and orders. Then went to another small island along the route and caught the sub "sailfish" which you've probably read about by now. It used to be called the Squalus you know and was rechristened. Anyway the whole thing was practically a repetition scene for scene of the sub "Copperfin" in that movie "Destination Tokyo" only we went toward Iwo Jima. Of course then, it didn't mean a thing at all to us. It was supposed to be occupied but no one had any inkling as to how heavily. This was all on D-Day minus four, or four days before the American invasion by the fifth marines. All five of us hunted up this Jap frequency that was sending coded messages and copied it (all was in the Jap Katakana). And one of the other officers who was a cryptograph specialist, got out his machines and tried to break it down, and succeeded right away. We worked on the sub all the time in pitch black night for about 18 hours and never a patrol plane or ship came within sound of our radar. Then we got back out of sight and headed back along the same route and sent out the messages we had broken down, only in our own codes back to HQ at Guam. Really very dull which was very much to our liking. So far they warned us never to breathe a word to our closest friend or relative. The only one here who knows about it is my commanding officer at the school.

We did the identical same thing at Okinawa on D minus three. All this took place in a grand total of 8 days from start to finish, so out of my eight months overseas today I haven't had a bad deal at all. Of course now all the fighting is over so all I have to worry about now is getting a ship, which I'm not going to like at all. That is, I don't think I will. By the way, if you've recovered yet. I wouldn't have Pink and Pat put in the paper or anything. It's OK to tell anyway you want to, but people have been court marshaled for letting out information ahead of time and I really haven't permission from intelligence to have it published. They always give permission in a written form for special missions, like that. Anyway, I'm proud of it, because I really think we did a lot of good. That's about all the story. I'll tell you the details when I get home. Well so far this hasn't been much about recent happenings. Went on liberty Sunday and went to church. I didn't go to the dinner afterwards tho—had quite a crowd due to V-J day worship so decided to keep out of the road. Didn't do much else except to go to a show at Kaimuki Theatre.

Murray

I couldn't believe it. My father *had* written about his code breaking. Over the course of our journey, he'd convinced me that there was no use looking for it. He was sure he hadn't written about it. But there it was.

I marveled at his memory. The stories he'd told me months ago, decades after the war, were identical. The only thing that was missing was Mal. He'd written about everything surrounding Mal's death, but Mal himself wasn't anywhere to be found. I continued to read his letters, but Mal's name never came up.

My father continued to write letters home on a regular basis. But there wasn't much to write about now. The war was over, and his family anxiously awaited his return. Just as predicted, the office was almost completely cleared out when he finally had enough points to go home.

After two years in the service, and finally on his way home, he walked into a diner, ordered a meal, and looked around. He was struck by one thought: no one knew what he'd been through. The family sitting at the table next to his was eating their dinner, never knowing they were sitting next to someone who was just back from the war.

When he got home, he hung his uniform in the closet, and his memories stayed there too. There wasn't a huge celebration. Like most soldiers, he simply wanted to get back to the life he'd left. And after a home-cooked meal and a quiet celebration at home, he did just that.

Ironically, the job he worried would be taken by the woman who'd replaced him during the war was taken by a veteran who had more points and seniority. So instead, he was given a railroad job in Walla Walla, Washington.

A few years passed before his mother gave him the two notebooks full of his letters. He stored them away like any other book on the shelf. And that promise he'd made to his folks, that he would tell them more when he got home, never happened. It just didn't seem important anymore.

CHAPTER THIRTY-TWO

Intentional Time of Remembrance

MURRAY W. FISHER

To you who answered the call of your country and served in its Armed Forces to bring about the total defeat of the enemy, I extend the heartfelt thanks of a grateful Nation. As one of the Nation's finest, you undertook the most severe task one can be called upon to perform. Because you demonstrated the fortitude, resourcefulness and calm judgment necessary to carry out that task, we now look to you for leadership and example in further exalting our country in peace.

Harry Truman

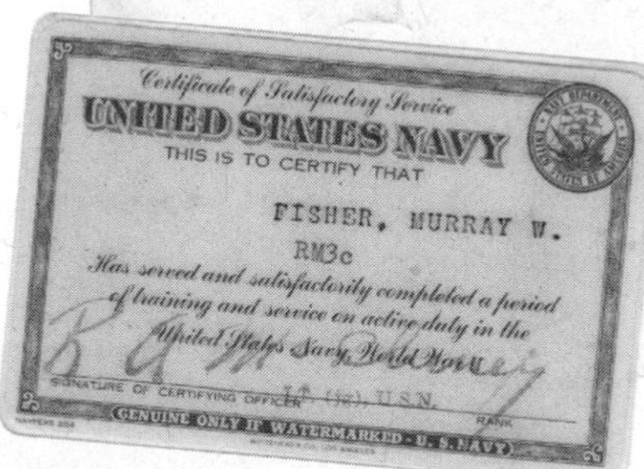

Certificate of Satisfactory Service

UNITED STATES NAVY

THIS IS TO CERTIFY THAT

FISHER, MURRAY W.

RM3c

Has served and satisfactorily completed a period of training and service on active duty in the United States Navy, World War II

SIGNATURE OF CERTIFYING OFFICER — Lt. (jg), U.S.N. — RANK

GENUINE ONLY IF WATERMARKED - U.S. NAVY

After so many years of war, it's hard to believe the fighting is all over and peace is here again.—August 10, 1945

I knew Dad would be at his men's Bible study, so I walked over to talk to my mom. She heated a cup of coffee for herself and made me a cup of tea. I leaned against the kitchen counter while we waited for the hot water.

"I'm still worried about Dad," I said.

"I know. I am too," she said.

We sat at the kitchen table. Just outside the window, below the fence, was the top of a twenty-foot retaining wall. Below, Mill Creek ran wildly. Whenever temperatures were unseasonably warm, run-off from the Blue Mountains would cause the creek to overflow. If we'd opened the window, the roar of it would have made it impossible to hear each other.

We sipped our hot drinks without talking. Then Mom broke the silence.

"You know," she said. "A few years after we got married, in maybe 1951 or 1952, I looked out the window and saw these two guys coming up the walk. They wore black suits and white shirts and stiff ties. They were FBI men. They asked for your dad. When he came to the door, they told him that he was now released to talk about what he did during the war."

"Really?" I asked.

She wrapped her hands around the coffee cup and stared at the raging water below.

"Yes," she said. "And that was the last we heard of it."

"Did he have nightmares or anything back then?" I asked.

She shook her head.

"He didn't," she replied. "I do remember that once I startled him and he said never to do that again. That was out of character for him. But other than that, I never saw any signs that anything was wrong."

"So many veterans talk about being jumpy or hitting the ground when they hear a car backfire," I said. "But for him, I think it was just put on a shelf, like the notebooks."

She looked at me then.

"And those notebooks," my mother said. "You know they sat on that same shelf all those years. I knew they were there. But I just moved them every now and then, dusted, and put them back." Her demeanor changed.

"You didn't have any reason to think any more about them," I tried to reassure her. "Why would you?"

She looked down.

"It wouldn't have mattered anyway," I said. "I feel like the timing was just right. You know? This was meant to come to the surface now."

She nodded.

As a child I hadn't really wanted to listen to his stories. Then I went to college, got married, and had three children. If he'd hinted at something or mentioned it in passing, my life was so crazy busy that I probably wouldn't have caught on. If there was a right time for things like this, then this was probably it.

"Yes," my mother said. "God's timing is perfect."

"You know, Mom," I said, "this whole thing has really tested my faith. There are times when he is hurting so much and I just don't understand. If God is so good, why would He allow Dad to remember such painful things so late in life? I mean, why not just let him live out his life in peace?"

It seemed cruel, unfair. He had lived for decades without being haunted by this. But now, when he was the least able to deal with the nightmare he'd lived through, there it was. It didn't make sense to me.

"But he never *was* at peace," my mother said. "Even before this, there was always something wrong. I could sense this wall he'd built up around himself. And through the years it got higher, thicker. He never let anyone get close—until now."

"But he's not at peace any more now than he was before," I said. "It seems like all of this was for nothing."

"It wasn't for nothing," she said sitting up straighter. "It wasn't for nothing. Maybe this is just a piece of it, this telling of his story. But there is more to come. I just want him to find peace. I want him to die in peace."

Unlike my father, my mother talked often about her own mortality. She gave things away and got on a list for a retirement home. She worried about the three of us girls having to go through the process of cleaning out the house when they were gone.

Dad was on the opposite end of the spectrum. He'd have nothing to do with talk of death or dying. I wondered if it was possible for him to change now.

"I told the men at my Bible study about Mal," my father said the next Wednesday.

"Really?" I asked.

"Yeah. We were ready to leave and I asked if anyone knew what PTSD was. No one did, except for our minister, Chuck Hindman. So then I shared the whole story. You could have heard a pin drop," he said.

It was the first time he'd shared the story with his friends.

"Of course," I replied. "It's quite a story, Dad. Did you tell them about breaking the code?"

"Yes," he said. "I told them about the whole thing, even about Mal. And then when everyone else left, Chuck asked me about it. He asked if he could come over and talk about it. I told him that you were writing my story. Would you want to come over for that?"

"Sure," I said.

The whole journey we'd taken together seemed to have drained him. It hadn't had the effect I'd hoped for. I wanted him to have peace. Maybe his minister could help.

We met in my parents' living room. Chuck took out a notebook and sat in the chair closest to my father. My mom and I sat on the sofa, listening. He asked my father lots of questions and wrote down his answers. Chuck thought of things I hadn't. He asked where Mal had been hit. I was surprised to learn that he'd been hit in the forehead—I had assumed it was in the chest. He asked about the relationship between my father and Mal. Dad had a hard time remembering some things, but other times his memory was vivid.

I just sat and listened. I didn't understand what exactly it was that Chuck was doing. *Will he want to go outside by the flagpole and say a prayer?* I wondered. *Will we have some kind of a ceremony when he is finished?* But he just took notes.

He concluded by thanking my father for sharing the story of his friendship with Mal. Dad smiled. I thanked him as he stood, still unsure of what exactly was going on. When Chuck walked to the door, I followed him. Mom and Dad were talking about something briefly, so I asked him what would come next.

"Well, I'm going to go home and type this up," he said. "I've done this with many, many people, Karen," the minister said. "I've found that there's healing in having an intentional time of remembrance. During war, there isn't time to stop and remember the one that has passed. When veterans come back from war, even today, setting aside some time to remember those they've lost can make a big difference. I've seen it time and again. It's healthy. Dealing with death is part of living."

"That's interesting," I said. "I've never thought about it that way. I'm sure you're right."

"Since you are the keeper of the memories," he said, "can I email what I write up to you?"

"Sure," I said.

A few days later, it arrived. And I understood. He wrote the words that a pastor or minister might say at a funeral. He wrote them just as he would for someone who had just died. But this memorial, typed and sent through email, was more than sixty years after Mal's death. Somehow, in those few hours we were together, Chuck had understood. He had really understood.

But the memorial needed a place to be read. I thought about the places around Walla Walla where we could do a memorial for Mal. The Blue Mountains were just a short distance away, but there was probably a few feet of snow at this time of year.

I thought about the flagpole he'd erected in memory of Mal. But even that didn't seem quite right. Over the next few days, I couldn't get one very specific place out of my mind: Hawaii.

I called my mom one afternoon.

"I wish he'd go back to Hawaii," I said. "We could do some kind of a memorial for Mal."

"Well that's one thing he won't agree to," she said. "The trip would be too hard on him. But I'll pray about it."

While my mother prayed, my sister Susan and I worked on Dad. Susan sent him emails and talked to him on the phone. I did the same. I couldn't stop thinking about it. It was just a feeling, but it was a strong feeling. This might be the only chance my father had at living out his days in peace. He was eighty-five years old.

Dad, as predicted, wasn't agreeable to the idea. There was no point arguing that the trip would not be difficult for him. His back often hurt when he sat for more than an hour, let alone five hours on a cramped plane. He'd been having more and more trouble walking any distance at all, so what would he do in Hawaii if he couldn't walk very far? His arguments were logical. They made complete sense. But I couldn't shake the strong feeling that this was his chance.

Finally, I decided to have a heart-to-heart with him. I walked over to his house, rehearsing what I'd say to him. But when I got there, I just spoke from the heart.

"Dad," I said, "when you first gave me the letters you wrote to your folks, I never imagined what I'd learn about you. When I decided to transcribe them, that's all I was going to do. I just wanted my kids to each have a copy. But something happened along the way. Slowly, you told me the real story. And that real story included your friend Mal. I feel like he's a part of our family now."

My father leaned back in his chair and closed his eyes. A tear ran down his cheek.

"I've watched you when you were sad. I know you feel guilty that you survived and Mal didn't. But you didn't get a chance to just stop and remember Mal. You were in the middle of a war. Mal died and you were whisked off to the hospital. That's not the way it's supposed to be. We can't grieve properly without stopping everything to take the time to do it. You couldn't do that during the war. But you can do it now. I want to be there with you when you do."

My father leaned forward, taking a handkerchief from his pocket. He held it to his face.

"I know it'll be a hard trip for you, Dad. Susan knows that and Mom knows that. But we'll do everything we can to make it the best it can be for you. You don't have to say anything at all right now. I just wanted you to know why I think this is so important."

I stood to leave and then turned around.

"I love you, Dad," I said.

I left then. I walked out the door and down the street. I held my emotions in check until I opened the door to my house. Then I sobbed like a baby.

I hoped he'd call or come by that night but he didn't. I went to bed that night with a heavy heart. My husband tried to console me.

"You did everything you could," he said.

But even after all this time, I still felt like I could have done more.

The next morning my mother called.

"Your father wants to go to Hawaii," she said.

My father, the man who said he'd never go back to Hawaii again, had a change of heart. In the chaos of planning the trip, I didn't have time to share the memorial that the minister had written up. But I printed off three copies as I scrambled to make arrangements for the house and the husband and children I'd be leaving behind. My sister Susan planned to go too and worked feverishly to make the travel arrangements for us.

We left Walla Walla on a bleak, cold day in January. Five hours later, my mother, father, sister, and I stepped off the plane in Hawaii.

CHAPTER THIRTY-THREE

Never Good-Bye

I'm proud of it, because I really think we did a lot of good. That's about all the story.—September 2, 1945

Susan and I shared a room right across from Waikiki beach. Mom and Dad were right next door. We all enjoyed the same incredible view.

Within a day or two, we'd all settled into our vacation routine. We met for breakfast each morning to plan our days. Most of the time that meant that the three girls would meet at the beach and Dad would go down too, sitting on a park bench nearby. Our hotel was right across the street, so Dad could walk down and read a book. When we got too hot, we'd go sit by Dad for a while or we'd all go get an ice cream cone. Most nights we'd eat dinner together. It was a very relaxed routine compared to my chaotic life at home. In between sunbathing and swimming in the ocean, we went our own ways: shopping, walking, reading, napping.

On Wednesday, Dad and I even had our weekly meal together, at Cheeseburger in Paradise. But time was running out and we still hadn't done anything about a memorial. Every time I brought the subject up, my father brushed it off. He said that it was enough that we were all there together. He said that it didn't matter.

I knew that wasn't true. Susan and I kept talking about it in our room at night. We finally decided that we'd have to make the decision for him.

On Saturday night, I knocked on my parents' door. Susan followed.

"We're going to do the memorial tomorrow morning," I said.

"Oh, you don't have to do that. It's good enough that we're all here together," he protested.

After talking for a few minutes, he finally said he'd think about it. But back in our room, Susan and I decided that one way or another, we had to make it happen.

We met for breakfast the next morning.

"I guess it will be OK to do the memorial for Mal," Dad said.

I held back tears, suddenly realizing how hard this would be for him.

It was Sunday morning, church day, that we walked down to the pier together. When he got tired along the way, we stopped so he could rest on a bench that faced the ocean. When he stood back up, he turned and our eyes met for just a moment. But in that short moment, I saw something I hadn't seen before. It had been years since we started this journey—years since he'd drawn a line in the sand. Every time I stepped over that line, he'd somehow gotten further away. But now I saw something different, something new. I stepped over the line he'd drawn so long ago. I was a little girl again. I slipped my tiny hand into his and we walked away together.

When we reached the pier, we walked the rest of the way in silence. The sounds of vacationing tourists filled the air. Children laughed as they joked with each other. People chatted happily. Tourists and sunbathers were scattered at the end of the pier. A tanned native Hawaiian woman sat on the cement ledge with her primitive fishing pole, threading line through her toes.

"Why don't we sit here," I said.

Mom and Dad sat on the low, cement wall. As activity swirled around us, my mom, sister, and I took turns reading the words the minister had written. Dad was hearing them for the first time.

In Loving Memory of Mal

1925–1945

We don't know his full name, and the mental picture of him has faded over the decades, but Mal remains indelibly in the mind of his best buddy over sixty years after his tragic death. Because war is so intense and demanding, there may never have been a funeral or other memorial for him, even though he made a tremendous contribution to the war effort. At best, there was a burial at sea, a world away from his family and childhood friends. Therefore, it seems fitting to remember him now.

The first time his friend Murray Fisher remembers meeting Mal was when they were both stationed in Hawaii. They were assigned to the top-secret duty of copying Japanese code so it could be fed into a machine that would break it into understandable words. Their particular group was composed of several young men. Their duty was so secret and essential to the war effort that their instructor told them they would be put in solitary confinement for the rest of the war if they were caught talking to each other or anyone else about what they were doing. If they were found to have shared information that got back to the Japanese, they would be shot without a court martial. They knew that agents were probably keeping an eye on them almost constantly for fear of blowing one of the most important secrets of the war. As a result, their friendship had to grow without the normal conversations about their work together, which made it easier for them to share little even about their past or their families. At the same time, though, the bonds of being in the war together and sharing the code of silence brought a special attachment. After all, how many other soldiers would understand what they were experiencing?

They went through training and leave together. They shared training in jungle warfare and language school. They went to movies and to the beach together, and Murray still remembers going to Mary's Steak House where Mary once made up a special batch of strawberry shortcake just for them. That was as near to home as a sailor could get.

When the battle of Iwo Jima broke out, however, Mary's became a distant memory. They were placed aboard a submarine equipped with a top-secret antenna which allowed them to receive code without being on the surface. They stayed at their stations almost constantly for fear of missing communication that could be critical to the war effort. Later they did the same thing at Okinawa. When the code-receiving equipment aboard their new submarine broke, they were transferred by raft to a ship, the flagship of a fleet which was bristling with antennas and other electronic equipment. But the station below deck also had problems, so they were taken topside so that they could plug in their equipment and continue their work. By the time they boarded the ship, every window was gone. They stayed a few miles off Okinawa for several days, copying code almost around the clock.

The day of the kamikaze attack, things turned into hell on earth. It was the most concentrated kamikaze attack of the war, with hundreds of planes blackening the sky on their way to the completion of their suicide missions. Every gun in the fleet was firing constantly and U.S. fighters were shooting down as many Japanese as possible, but their ship took its share of hits. The Japanese knew it was an important target because of its size and the number of antennas. Mal and Murray stayed at their stations, copying code constantly as the battle raged. Murray remembers burning a finger when he reached down to touch a piece of shrapnel that had imbedded in an ammunition box on which he was seated.

Murray had just traded places with Mal when a kamikaze crashed into the water and shrapnel struck Mal in the forehead, fatally wounding him. His last words were "Oh, Murray!" before he lost consciousness. As is often the case in war, no one knows why some are hit and others are not. Murray's wounds were psychological. The next thing he remembers is waking up in the hospital.

We will never know if Mal ever had a fitting memorial. Without a full name, tracing his records is near impossible. Typically, sailors lost in such battles were buried at sea along with others who did not survive. What we do know is that Mal was a fine young man with a bright mind who served in one of the most vital tasks of the war in the Pacific. He died in battle, faithfully serving his country almost until his last breath. It is fitting that he continue to be honored for the service he gave and the life he sacrificed.

As Christians, we believe that Mal's life did not end as he breathed his last breath, but rather it entered into eternal life—the "peace that passes all understanding." In the words of St. Paul, the tent maker, "If the earthly tent we have is destroyed, we have a building not made with hands, eternal in the heavens." We also trust that Christ's spirit was there with them on the deck of the ship, even as the hell of war was raging around them. We know that the one who suffered and died on a cross also grieves with us when a friend is taken away. In the words of the psalmist, "Even if I make my bed in hell, thou art there."

O Lord, again we give to you Mal's life that was taken away so tragically by the whims of war. As you have received him into eternal life, lead us also in your paths until that day when we shall all meet again. In Jesus's name we pray. Amen.

When we finished reading, I slowly became aware of our surroundings. At first I thought it just seemed quiet because we were so focused. But looking up now, I could see that everything around us had changed. The jovial tourists were now solemn. Children held their parents' hands. Some had bowed their heads. Others stood silently watching. Even the native woman had pulled her line from the ocean in quiet respect.

This wasn't a perfect memorial. It wasn't private. It didn't allow us space to grieve. But the people there that day stood in the gap of what was lacking. Without knowing what they were a part of, each stepped into their role effortlessly. And I was reminded that war stops for no one. Men were buried in the midst of war without a service. They were buried without ashes and dust. So perhaps this too, this imperfect service, was as it should be. We could feel the holy ground we stood on, all around us.

I opened the clear container and handed the flower lei to my father.

"I don't know what to do," he said.

"Just slide them off into the water," I said.

He looked down at the water and then out at the horizon. He slid a flower into the water below. He handed it to me. I did the same and then my sister and my mother. We took turns gently dropping the flowers onto the water. Against the current, the flowers made their way, as if following an unpaved road, out to sea.

A teenager and his father were on surfboards in the water below. They were divided by the path of flowers. When the teen unknowingly started to swim through it, his father put his hand up. The boy looked at the flowers and then up at the elderly man on the pier. Father and son watched as each petal floated out to sea.

"They're going to Okinawa," my father said softly.

I nodded. He said something else, but it was a whisper.

Then he turned. I watched as my father walked away, tears warming my eyes. I looked back at the red and white flowers on the sea below.

"He never forgot you," I whispered. "Rest in peace, Mal."

The day before we left Hawaii, a storm hit the island. All of the shops closed their massive glass doors. The busy streets were now virtually deserted, only a few people venturing out. I stood on the balcony of our hotel room watching as the wind picked up anything not fastened down and tossed it swirling down the streets and into the air. Every bush, branch, and foliage shook. But it was two palm trees that caught my attention.

They stood together in the sunshine, away from the rest, and were blown from side to side with the violent force of the wind. But the remarkable thing was that only the palm branches moved. The base of the trees remained strong. I went inside the hotel room to get my camera. When I came back, something had changed.

The sun had shifted so that one of the trees was now in darkness, shaded. The other remained illuminated by the sun. I thought about my father and Mal, and the battles they'd fought. Mal's had been fought during war. My father's began as he held his dying friend in his arms. Something profound happened as he felt life leave his friend. He carried it with him for more than fifty years, never letting light penetrate that dark, dark place. But as he remembered his friend, with flowers that pushed against the tides toward Okinawa, light slowly penetrated the darkness.

My father had finally found peace.

A few days later, an old man stood in the silence of the morning. Peace surrounded him as he gazed up at the flag erected in memory of his friend and comrade. He gently held each flower in his aged hand before placing them, one-by-one, at the base of it.

"When we were in Hawaii, did you say good-bye to Mal?" I asked.

He looked down, shook his head.

"Never good-bye," he said. "Just...see you later."

Afterword

If this book had been published within the year after the memorial in Hawaii, it would have had a "happily ever after" ending. I've come to believe in the power of an intentional time of remembrance and the peace it can bring. For an entire year, my father didn't have a single nightmare or flashback. He described the time at the end of the pier as a peace he just can't explain. He held on to that peace for a year.

But then the symptoms of PTSD slowly crept back in.

Many of our veterans suffer from the traumas of war long after they've left the battlefield, and their wounds are every bit as deep as a physical wound. Although it would have been nice to end the book on a happy note, that is not reality. The wounds of war may never completely heal. But joy and peace can still be realized. That is my wish for veterans today.

The comrade referred to as Jonesy in so many of my father's letters was never seen again after my father returned from Okinawa.

Thomas Coldwell (not his real name), the man whose life my father saved, returned from the war. He married and had children and grandchildren. He never knew what my father did for him.

We sent for my father's military records. A lot, but not all, of what he did during the war was contained in them. While this is a big disappointment to my father, I still believe that it is possible to have peace without all the pieces. If my father found it once, he can find it again. As he recently joked, "Maybe I'll just have to go to Hawaii every year."

My father never found out why there was an office set up for him, as if he worked there every day. It remains a mystery.

For the veterans whose stories remain untold, I hope this book is a beacon. Our WWII veterans are dying at a rate of more than a thousand every day. Each day draws us closer to a time when there will no longer be anyone who can tell us firsthand what their experiences were.

Post-traumatic stress is real. Although there is more awareness for today's veterans, help is often sporadic and sorely lacking. When we send our young men and women to fight a war while we stay home enjoying the freedom they're fighting for, we owe them whatever it takes to make them whole again. Whether the veteran returned from war sixty years ago or six days ago, one thing remains constant: it's time for us to talk and to listen.

About the Author

Photograph by Kimberly Miner

Karen Fisher-Alaniz is an author and writer who began the journey of writing this memoir when her father handed her a collection of letters on his eighty-first birthday. She lives with her family in the Pacific Northwest.